IGNITION

How to start up a tech startup

Andreas Bauer
Julian Hall

Published in 2014
© Andreas Bauer & Julian Hall 2014

ISBN - 978-0-9926422-5-9
BISAC: Computers / Internet / World Wide Web

Design, layout & illustration by Jeremy Salmon
Marketing by Julian Hall

Foreword

Ialways call
myself an 'Accidental
Entrepreneur' and I also say I am not a techie,
and yet, I have been in the tech industry for 30 years, I
own my own tech company, and I have a share in five other
companies. Being asked to write the foreword to this excellent
book brought a smile to my face; I feel very privileged. It is in the
title, How to Start Up a Tech Startup…what a brilliant title with a clear
intention. I wish I had read this 15 years ago!

Without doubt we are in the Digital Era; no single company can ignore the
impact of digital. No one can hide; no business owner or Board Director can
delegate this subject to the IT Department. Digital is not a sector and it is not the
domain of a few tech companies; this is as basic to business now as understanding
finance and marketing. The casualties that sit in the "Do you remember that
company called XXX?" zone show the signs of many Boards that could not adapt
to a new age of communication, service, and delivery mechanisms. How exciting
that you are considering a startup at this time.

I asked Andreas and Julian why they were writing this book and what their
intention was, and their reply was "That when someone has read this book
they will be more successful in fundraising, winning in the marketplace,
and growing." A fine place to start when you write a book.

Over the 15 years that I have worked with startups, the
mindset and tenacity of the Founder has always
been the biggest hurdle for a startup.

There are now nearly 30 million small businesses in the US and 4.9 million companies in the UK alone, and as we know, we are in a global marketplace now so the competition is greater than ever before. But who are your competition? We can no longer look directly at those who provide exactly the same product or service; we are in a far greater marketplace than that, we are in an Attention War. There are so many things we can all spend our money on: products, services, apps, software, devices, experiences, the list goes on and on. So your mindset and commitment to your startup has to be bulletproof. It is all too easy to register a company and create a website now — the tough part starts when you join this Attention War. This is when your commitment to getting the skills to run a business takes over the clever part of knowing technology.

I have seen so many brilliant tech startups, awesome coders, and awesome techies who have an idea and set their sights on the millions they will earn by building it. 'Build it and they will come' has been the attitude of many failed businesses. We now have to be extraordinary networkers, we have to be passionate and share our enthusiasm, and we have to be amazing at business. The investors out there want to know 'Which sector are you going to disrupt?' In fact, I heard that the language in Silicon Valley is 'Who are you going to kill?' We have to be different, we have to know our market, we have to have massive empathy with our audience, we have to seek to heal problems and make life easier, better, happier, more fun, and know how to grow those followers that will amplify us and believe in us. Finally, we have to look over our shoulders all the time and keep innovating and developing, as this market is not static.

When I read this book I sensed a great deal of experience, empathy and a strong intention to coach and support you on your journey. Peer2Peer learning is the most powerful way to gain our knowledge, it is real, current, and has the guts to tell you how it is, from painful and honest experience. Andreas and Julian are standing right by you now.

I am so excited for anyone who is considering his or her own business. The adrenaline rushes through me imagining you starting this journey. My advice is never stop believing in what you felt when you first had that heartbeat of an idea. Many things will take you off course, many people will challenge your beliefs and your tenacity; it is not wrong to fail, but it is wrong not to try. In Steve Jobs words, "stay hungry, stay foolish" and from me "stay humble".

Penny Power OBE

Why this Book?

Venture Capitalists like to invest in fast-growing technology startups with energetic founders developing leading edge and highly promising technologies and selling it to the world. But the reality is that many entrepreneurs complain about a lack of funding and the mortality rate of tech startups is staggering. Is the equity gap really that deep that it leaves many startups out? Still, we know stories of companies that that were able to close massive funding rounds and create very successful businesses. What is it that sets them apart? What are they doing different? And what are their ingredients of success? There are many.

This book explores, by sharing our experience of working with startups for years, what investors are looking for and unravels some of the myths behind venture investments. Investment readiness is not only about preparing a fantastic pitch and business plan, it is about getting the various elements right — elements that determine the success of the company. It is about your technology and product, about marketing and selling it, about fundraising, and last but not least about execution and having the right team to do so.

We sincerely hope that as many entrepreneurs as possible have the opportunity to read this book and learn from the stories we tell for their own benefit. There are voices that say that great startups always find money, and money always funds great startups. But still, fundraising is one of the most crucial activities in the life of an entrepreneur, and getting the elements right and becoming investment ready is key.

It is also our desire to get investors exposed to better investment opportunities. Ill-prepared entrepreneurs and underfunded startups are in nobody's interest. What can be more sad than a tech startup with a great product and enthusiastic founders who cannot live up to their full potential or fail because they are underfunded? Investors also greatly benefit from improved deal flow with well-prepared startups.

We hope you enjoy reading our essays and apply some of the lessons from our stories to your tech startup. This is how you get the most out of it.

What to Expect !

This book has been written for anyone interested
or involved with technology startups: founders,
employees, investors, advisors, board members,
service providers, and anyone who plans to start up
his own startup, such as entrepreneurs or students
who choose the startup business as their career path
or as a second career after retirement.

We have tried to highlight some concepts which we
believe are important for the success of any tech
startup, and have summarized them in short and
easy to read essays based on our own experience
in working with startups for many years. Each essay
is self-contained, and where necessary or helpful
we included references to related concepts we have
introduced in other chapters.

Throughout the book, we use the masculine gender
to refer to both genders equally for the sole reason of
making reading easier, without intent to express any
preference.
We hope you enjoy reading this book and find its
information helpful.

Please provide us with feedback by going to
www.TheIgnitionBook.com

The authors
Andreas Bauer
Julian Hall

Content

One: On Technology and Product

Two: On Marketing and Sales

Three: On Funding and Fundraising

Four: On Team and Execution

ONE

On Technology
and Product

Build It and They Will Come
Or Will They?

According to the Netcraft January 2014 Web Server Survey there are over 861 million websites that exist on the web. Apple announced recently that 1 million apps reside on their app store. Google Play, which provide apps for the Android platform boast similar numbers if not more!

But with figures like that it is no wonder the landscape of dot-com and app based businesses is littered with failures — lots of them. But why is that? With the runaway successes of so many technology companies, do you not just build it and they come?

Yes and no.

Who remembers MySpace? Vaguely? Yeah me too!

Originally built to service the music industry, it wasn't too long before almost everyone had an account (active or inactive) on MySpace. Its meteoric rise to success was a testament to the resurgence of the dot-com sector and there was a time when it was hard to believe their reign would come to an end. But it did. Even though MySpace didn't have an Achilles heel as such, there were quite a few reasons why after they built it, people came…and then they left, many of which are due to what Facebook did right.

Hands up if you use WhatsApp? All of you? Yeah me too!

On their blog the WhatsApp founders posted:

"Almost five years ago we started WhatsApp with a simple mission: building a cool product used globally by everybody. Nothing else mattered to us.

Today we are announcing a partnership with Facebook that will allow us to continue on that simple mission. Doing this will give WhatsApp the flexibility to grow and expand, while giving me, Brian, and the rest of our team more time to focus on building a communications service that's as fast, affordable and personal as possible.

Here's what will change for you, our users: nothing."

Now here's the thing. The focus must be on the users, not making money or investor returns. Keep the users 'using' and the rest follows. Simple.

Build it and they will come only works if once the users are there you listen and listen well. After you've listened, watch. What do we mean? Well, almost each time Facebook has made a major change, be it adverts, timeline, graph search, etc., people complained en masse but continued to use the platform, got used to the change, and life went on. People aren't built for change, even if the change is for the better. So monitor user behavior on your technology to monitor what people are actually doing, as opposed to what they're saying. Sometimes the two will marry, sometimes they won't.

Forbes Magazine said "...the brilliance of Mark Zuckerberg was his willingness to allow Facebook to go wherever the market wanted it."

Finally, look at 'White Space Management'. According to Wikipedia "...the White Space as described by Geary A. Rummler and Alan P. Brache in 1991, is the area between the boxes in an organization chart or the area between the different functions: Very often no one is in charge or responsible for the White Space. The important handoffs between functions are happening here, and this is very often the area where an organization has the greatest potential for improvements. In the White Space things often "fall between the cracks" or "disappear into black holes", resulting in misunderstandings and delays. To manage the White Spaces is a way to improve process performance of an organization."

Adam Hartung, Author of Create Marketplace Disruption: How to Stay Ahead of the Competition, says: "And that's the nature of White Space management. No rules. Not really any plans. No forecasting markets. Or foretelling uses. No trying to be smarter than the users to determine what they shouldn't do. Not prejudging ideas so as to limit capability and focus the business toward a projected conclusion. To the contrary, it was about adding, adding, adding and doing whatever would allow the marketplace to flourish. Permission to do whatever it takes to keep growing. And resource it as best you can – without prejudice as to what might work well, or even best. Keep after all of it. What doesn't work stop resourcing, what does work do more."

It is the user who is in the driver's seat, and he or she is the ultimate judge of market success. Try to learn from their behaviour as much as you can; the success of your tech depends on it.

What Problem Does the Product Solve?

It is the user who is in the driver's seat, as we have seen in a previous chapter. But guess what happens more often than you might imagine? Figure this...

Many technology startup founders have a background in technology. Even more, they have a passion for technology. This is key for them to embark on a cruel journey to get a company off the ground from zero and grow it into a major player. However, many founders unfortunately run the risk of falling in love with the technology and product they develop. They forget that it is the market where the rubber meets the road. Developing products that do not resolve any real user problem or satisfy a user desire is doomed to commercial failure.

Likewise, developing products that appeal only to early adopters won't make them a commercial success. A product eventually needs to achieve mass-market appeal.

Even worse, there are many real problems out there that call for a solution, but nobody seems to care or is willing to put in an effort to address them. There are all kinds of barriers to adoption, a topic that we will address in the next chapter.

So what is a startup supposed to do? First, start with a why. There needs to be a real problem to be solved or a real desire to be satisfied. Only then will a customer be willing and happy to buy and pay for the product. The key here is that the problem or desire needs to be real in the mind of the customer, not just made up in the mind of the entrepreneur. And it must be painful or desirable enough for the customer to take action.

There are certainly many problems out there that might be very real, but nobody takes any action. People simply won't bother. And there are many desires that are more like aspirations and wishful thinking, and people intuitively are aware and don't take action.

Now, how can an entrepreneur tell that a problem or desire is real and users will act? It's very simple; he has to ask the customer. That's the way to do it; the only way. Certainly, this field research can be complemented by studies of market trends that provide additional and often very valuable insight. Also, asking the customer is not a one-off affair, it is a permanent process that starts with testing the waters with the very first idea, and goes on and on and on through prototyping the first product with friendly customers, to seeking constant customer feedback, and product improvements after launch.

Many entrepreneurs believe therefore that it is a good idea to ask their friends for their opinion. Well, it isn't. More often than not, friends don't like to give negative feedback. Imagine a product is useless — what would the entrepreneur's friends say? It is much better to ask the man on the street who is not emotionally attached. It doesn't really matter what your friends think. What matters is what your future customers think.

And that is one of the fundamental principles behind a lean startup: get real feedback, fail fast, and pivot early.

Barriers to Adoption and Barriers to Entry

We hear it all the time: "My product is first to market." "My business is so unique that is has no competitor." "I have a first-mover advantage." That's all great, but:

There are many aspects to consider.

Being first-to-market is not necessarily a prerequisite to becoming the market leader. Google was not first-to-market in search engines, several others were there before them. Markets are not always mature enough to adopt a startup's new product and the first mover has to bear the brunt, cost, and effort of educating and making the market. And first movers can get outpaced by late movers with better solutions or more money in their pockets, which they spend on marketing to achieve leadership in a market that was educated and built with the first mover's money.

What is important in this context is to taker a close look at two interrelated concepts: Barriers to adoption and barriers to entry. And these are concepts venture capitalists study closely.

Barriers to Adoption

The question the entrepreneur has to answer is not "Why would a customer buy my product?" but "What would hold the customer back from buying my product?" There can be many reasons. Here are some:

- No real problem. The product might solve a perceived problem, but nobody really cares. Nobody bothers taking action; everyone seems to have become used to the problem and just lives with it.

- Too painful. The product might solve a problem, but adopting it might require an effort that customers are not willing to make. It is less painful to suffer the problem than to adopt the solution.

- Fear of the unknown. Many people suffer from this syndrome. They don't want to adopt a new product unless they fully understand it and are convinced of their benefits, or after others have started using it.

- Unwillingness to change habits. That is the "It has always been like this" syndrome.

- Lack of enthusiasm. This occurs more often then we might think. Many people simply don't get excited by new technologies.

Barriers to Entry

This is an important concept for all tech startups and businesses in general, but above all for those that want to maintain a first-mover advantage. Being first-to-market doesn't mean that the startup has its first-mover advantage guaranteed for a lifetime. It is the company's obligation to erect and raise barriers to entry to protect the business against competitive threats and intrusions. Those barriers can come in many forms, for instance...

- User groups or social networks. This is the example of Facebook or LinkedIn. Once someone has many contacts or followers, he doesn't want to switch to an alternative provider.

- Proprietary technology creating vendor lock-in. Some examples are Apple iTunes or Amazon Kindle. Once the user has built a library of content, he will think twice about switching to another platform.

- Contractual obligations. This is a typical mechanism used for subscription-based services where the customers gets discounts or perks for signing multi-month or multi-year contracts and switching before expiration comes with a steep penalty.

- Loyalty programmes, gamification, and recommendations. This is about keeping the customer constantly engaged and rewarded for buying more.

- Exclusivity agreements. These agreements are used to lock in distribution channels or franchisees to your brand and products.

- Best-price guarantee. This tool can be very powerful for companies that are cost leaders in their category.

There are many more. But market leaders also need to think about market exposure and reach. Get the best market exposure possible, the highest ranking on Google searches or the broadest distribution network, be easy to find on the Internet, use influencers to broaden market appeal and get their "social proof", and many others. Unless you do that, someone else will…and will eventually become the leader.

Now let's move on to discuss the role of differentiation within the concept of first-mover advantage.

First-Mover Advantage and Differentiation

We mentioned in the previous chapter the importance of having a first-mover advantage, and discussed the need and ways to keep it.

But not every successful company was a first mover, among them some of the most successful companies and undisputed market leaders in history. Google is a case in point. When Google was founded, there had already been several search engines in the market. What set Google apart was a new approach to searching that produced better results; a search not based on keywords, which was at that time the common approach. And for monetization, Goggle used click ads rather than the prevalent banner ads which were then popular with advertisers but not with end users. Both pillars of success have been cornerstones of Google's success to this day.

What this example shows us is the power of differentiation to offset the lack of first-mover advantage. Let us elaborate on this. What does differentiation really mean?

Its basic concept is about being different. If your product is a complete commodity, your competitive advantage needs to base itself on being the cheapest provider or having the broadest market reach. However, as is the case with most tech startups, if the startup can gain competitive advantage through differentiation, it has to differentiate…but differentiate on aspects that do matter to the customer. Differentiation just to be different won't do the trick.

But how does an entrepreneur know what type of differentiation matters to the customer? There is only one way to find out: by asking the customer. It is to him to whom the differentiation needs to matter. This is the same concept that we described in a previous chapter on what problem the product solves. What matters are the customer's desires, problems, preferences, and tastes. Often entrepreneurs believe they can and should differentiate through features and functions. Their product should have more features and a wider functionality then their competitors'. Is that really so? Not necessarily. Let's look again at the example of Google. The homepage has only one feature and functionality: to enter the search term. It is the simplest interface anyone can imagine. Apple products are also known for their simplicity and ease of use and are not overloaded with too much functionality, which often is complicated to understand and adds only marginal value, if any at all. The lesson to learn here is that simplicity is key and overloading websites with features and functions can often backfire.

Let us also give you another word of caution: Differentiation is all good, but it makes sense only if your product gets found on the Internet or in the market place. If nobody knows about you and your product, nobody will buy from you despite all your differentiation. So don't forget to spend on marketing and sales; don't pump your entire budget into technology in order to differentiate.

On Technology Risk and Market Risk

Tech startups are a risky business. They develop brand new and often unproven technology for markets that are still be made, and do all that on a shoestring budget.

It is in the interest of the founders and investors to understand and minimize the risk involved.

There are several types of risk that need to be managed. Experts in the field typically distinguish between technology and market risk. Counter to intuition, it is often the market risk that creates havoc and causes a startup to fail. Let us look at the two types in detail.

Technology Risk

This is the risk of not getting the technology that is being developed to work or to do what it is supposed to do. Luckily, only few startups fail because of technology risk. Obviously, no one can defy the laws of science, but tech entrepreneurs usually manage the technology risk quite well, for a variety of reasons.

- Tech entrepreneurs often have a strong technology background and enjoy working on challenging, leading-edge technology projects.

- Technology development is well understood and follows a well-known and proven path, from developing a prototype or beta product to a commercial product that in turn will be improved over time following a well-defined technology roadmap.

- Technology development environments are usually controlled and sheltered from outside influence.

- Few people, often not even a handful, are involved in technology development.

- The Internet and availability of rapid development methods and tools has shortened development times significantly and allows the entrepreneur to fail fast and make adjustments quickly.

It is often where the rubber meets the road where the real risk becomes apparent. Therefore, specific attention needs to be paid to the market risk.

Market Risk

This is the risk of not being able to achieve adoption of the product in the marketplace. When you truly think about it, it becomes clear why market risk is often much higher than technology risk. Let us elaborate, using the same criteria as before.

- Tech entrepreneurs often have a strong technology background, but lack passion and skills in marketing and sales.

- Product launch and marketing is less understood and doesn't follow a well-known and proven path.

- The market is open, and the consumer is in full control.

- Many people are involved: the company employees, marketers, distribution channels, agents, and eventually the consumers, with no single point of control.

- The Internet and availability of rapid development methods and tools has shortened development times and costs significantly, with more startups than ever getting started, competing in the same market for the attention and wallet share of the same customers.

It is the market risk that needs to be managed carefully. Therefore, we have dedicated a separate chapter in the section On Marketing & Sales on this important topic. Because the truth is:

"Sales Cure All." - Mark Cuban

"Execution Is What Matters." - Andreas Bauer & Julian Hall

Pivoting Your Product and Staying Alive

If you have come across the word pivoting, you may already know that it is a key attribute for businesses, practiced by leading technology companies around the world. It simply means to start something, test it, and when it does not work, change direction to lead to a solid and successful deliverable. This is one of the most popular ways of making a technology product work. But there is more to pivoting and, as we can see from the diagram below, pivoting may outrun perseverance in the current generation of technology.

Pivot vs. Persevere

Pivot is a buzzword growing in use among startup founders, some of whom are finding investors, even after ditching their original business plans. Here's a look at some young tech companies that switched gears, compared to some others that persevered, or stuck to their original premise.

PIVOT

- **Groupon**, a daily-deals site launched in 2008, initially focused on using group dynamics to fundraise and was called ThePoint.
- **Twitter,** a microblogging and social platform unveiled in 2006, was originally a podcast-directory service called Odeo.
- **Instagram**, a mobile photo application launched in 2010, was formerly a mobile microblogging platform called Burbn.
- **OMGPOP**, a games site that Zynga acquired for $180 million in April 2012, started as dating site flirting site Iminlikewithyou in 2006.
- **Fab.com**, daily deal design site launched in 2011 was originally a gay social network.

PERSEVERE

- Facebook, launched as a social network in 2004 and reported 901 million active monthly users as of the end of March 2012, is preparing a highly anticipated initial public offering expected to be the largest Internet listing in history.
- Pinterest, launched in 2009 as a website that allows users create online scrapbooks to share images of projects or coveted products.
- Dropbox, launched in 2008 as a web-based file hosting and storage company.
- LinkedIn, a business social network started in 2003, has stuck with its basic philosophy while continuing to diversify its business model.
- Airbnb, an apartment rental service started in 2007, has expanded to new geographic markets.
- Zynga, a social game developer and publisher launched in 2009, has increased the number and variety of games.

Source: Wall Street Journal Online, *'Pivoting' Pays Off for Tech Entrepreneurs,* April 2012.

How to Bounce Back with Pivoting

For a tech start-up, pivoting can give you great opportunities to get it right. Instagram is one of the best examples of pivoting. It initially started off as a micro-blogging site in 2010, but when it realized that it was failing, the company instantly went on to becoming a photo-sharing app for Facebook and smartphones. Hence, they not only caught up with the current trends, i.e. the smartphone platform, but they also completely revamped their idea in a way that made it important for youngsters in the coming years to be part of the Instagram community, just as Facebook did. Instagram survived the tech rat race through pivoting. Here is how you too can use pivoting to rework your ideas and guide them to success:

- If your current idea does not work, don't throw it out. There is more to learn from the details of why your idea does not work for customers than you can ever imagine. The insights are valuable, and knowing those insights may come in useful later.

- It is important to connect with your customers. You should never base your new idea on desk research alone. Find out what customers want at the base level; speak to them. Find out what their regular habits are.

- It is always better to fail early. So if your first testing on the product fails, it is cheaper to correct your course than after you had launched the product on a large scale, because you've made a smaller investment.

- When you shoot an arrow at the bullseye, you have to look at the bullseye and not the arrowhead to successfully reach the target. In our case, the product is your arrow but your target is the customer, so steer towards your customers and not your product.

- If you serve the competitive field of technology, you should not think that having an average product is a success. Something that works is not good enough; you have to create a product that thrives.

About Agile Development

Agile Software Development (ASD) is a set of methodologies for teams in tech companies to help fulfill the need for simplicity through flexibility while delivering a finished product. Agile software development concentrates on simplifying the processes involved, such as coding, testing, and even delivering functional bits of the software application when the product is ready for delivery. The objective of these methodologies is to make the necessary changes quickly, based on client inputs, and get approval in parts as the development process progresses, rather than delivering one large software application in a chunk, which you normally do when following the conventional 'waterfall' methodology.

The project management process in the case of agile development is completely based on regular inspection and adapting to the changes. This is more of a leadership philosophy about handling a team of software developers, which promotes teamwork. It is a set of practices that allows the delivery of the highest quality software, aligned to the customer's requirements and goals.

Hence, as opposed to the conventional methodologies, especially 'waterfall', you are dealing with four basic elements when you choose agile development:

- Individuals and interactions over processes and tools
- Working software over comprehensive documentation
- Customer collaboration over contract negotiation
- Responding to change over following a plan

Through agile development, you constantly gain opportunities to assess the course of your tech projects throughout the entire development lifecycle. This is possibly one of the best examples of pivoting.

Product Innovation 101

The biggest mistake when discussing innovation is that it is oftentimes confused with improvement. To innovate is a verb defined as "Make changes in something established, especially by introducing new methods, ideas, or products." The key word here is new as opposed to improving on something that already exists.

The problem with most companies, tech or otherwise, is that their understanding of innovation is limited to improving rather than doing something new. Now that we've got that out of the way, what are the key areas of product innovation that you should consider right now?

Real innovation isn't always the response to a customer need, because it is clear that we didn't ask for the iPhone or iPad, but Apple gave it to us anyway. They developed something new which wasn't a direct response to an articulated customer need but to existing product deficiencies. Smartphones were only being used by the tech savvy community, and tablets…well tablets were barely being used by anyone.

As defined by Wikipedia, "Innovation differs from invention in that innovation refers to the use of a better and, as a result, novel idea or method, whereas invention refers more directly to the creation of the idea or method itself."

"Innovation differs from improvement in that innovation refers to the notion of doing something different rather than doing the same thing better."

There are usually four area of potential innovation in your business:

Finance	Process	Offering	Delivery
(1) BUSINESS MODEL – How the enterprise makes money	**(3) ENABLING PROCESS** – Assembled capabilities you typically buy from others	**(5) PRODUCT PERFORMANCE** – Features and functionality	**(8) CHANNEL** – How you connect customers to your offering
(2) NETWORKING How your value chain and partners make your offering distinctive	**(4) CORE PROCESS** – Proprietary processes that add value	**(6) PRODUCT SYSTEM** - Extended system surrounding an offering	**(9) CUSTOMER EXPERIENCE** – How you create an integrated experience
		(7) SERVICE – How you service customers	**(10) BRAND** – How you express your value to customers

The need for innovation today is being driven by the fact that:

> *"Yesterday's solutions won't fix today's problems in tomorrow's world."*
> - Julian Hall

Consider these things:

Finance
Think about how you're charging for your product or service. Are you able to offer a subscription model against a one-off payment? Can you offer a free/lite version of your product or service and up-sell your customer to the premium offering?

Process
Are you replicating work across your team? What aspects of your day-to-day operations can you streamline so that you can improve service or product delivery?

Offering
Are your features and functions based on improving, inventing, or innovating? Use the definitions above to get closer to innovation.

Delivery
How do your customers get your product or service? Online, mobile, direct, through referrals, delivery partners, etc.

Coming to grips with some of these questions will help you embark on the innovation path.

To Outsource or Not to Outsource

As Shakespeare said, "That is the question!" And in today's world of tech it is a question that most startups grapple with. You see, your product is everything and the execution of such is critical to the success of your fledging company.

Do you outsource and manage the development over email and Skype or keep it in-house and manage the development over the developers' shoulders? What are the pros and cons? Let's see!

Outsource Pros

- **Talent.** The global marketplace has provided startups with immediate access to worldwide talent in an instant.

- **Well the cost!** That's the #1 reason to outsource, because it can be far cheaper than hiring local talent.

- **Mature market.** Outsourcing isn't a new thing or a fad, it's been happening for a very long time now. There are a number of very well-developed platforms out there, perfect for helping you find the right partners and people.

Outsource Cons

- **You can't see who you're hiring.** You may think 'so what?' Well, an associate of ours who hires almost everyone from outsourced platforms had hired a developer who turned out to be a hacker. The hacker went on to do what he does best and hack the associate's website knowing that he was safe behind the glass screen of his laptop.

- **Quality issues can abound when hiring outsourced developers.** Not because these guys or gals are poor quality, but unless you are skilled at writing a professional brief and managing project developers, a wide gap starts to appear between what you want and what they deliver.

- **Language barriers.** This is a biggie, especially when you're trying to express intent and considerations that may be considered 'local'.

- **Filtering.** If you've ever submitted a proposal on an outsource platform, then you know about the deluge of bidders promising you the moon. Alarm bells ring, as it all sounds a bit too good to be true.

In-House Pros

- Execution. We could be wrong, but if you look at the most successful tech companies going you'll find that they didn't outsource their development. Being able to manage a team that don't necessarily have to be sitting right next to you but is for all intents and purposes 'in-house' can make the development process much easier.

- **Communications**. Having a team in-house means you can work on stuff together, ideas can be bounced around in a very organic way, and it can sometimes bring out the best in a team.

- *Localization.* Being in the same town or city means your developers will have a better chance of understanding any local or social considerations.

- *Knowledge retention.* It is easier to retain the full knowledge of the technology by keeping at least the key developers in-house and retaining them through attractive retention mechanisms.

In-House Cons

- *Cost.* Hiring a team or even just one developer locally can cost 5 to 10 times as much as outsourcing. Locally, developers are not only in demand but also have high costs of living. You end up paying the price – literally.

- *Management.* If you're not good at managing real people, then this may reveal itself to be a challenge. Developers need direction and an equal amount of room to get the job done. Get this mix wrong and your product could be affected.

- *Choosing the 'right' people.* The reality is that sometimes startups give away equity to get developers onboard. The other reality is that those developers still have bills to pay and your project could be de-prioritized when a paycheck comes along. Having the 'right' people can prevent this kind of thing from happening. The worst thing is having the wrong people locked into your company through equity. You can find more insight in the section On Team and Execution.

So what have we learned?

Outsourcing is harder than it looks, but if you have the skills and experience to filter the good from the bad, clearly communicate your brief, and professionally manage the resource, then you should be fine.

In-house can get you a great product but at a cost. If you can afford it, good; if you can't, then there's more than one way to skin that cat (e.g. via equity), but only if you use the right people.

So ultimately the answer is what fits your startup given budget, skills set, and quality of product.

P.S. It is OK to mix and match! Lots of successful projects have been completed with frontend development being done in-house and backend development being handled by an outsource outfit.

Technology for Equity
DOs and DON'Ts

Somebody once said, "You get what you pay for." This is true, but what they didn't say is when you need to pay for it. The technology sector is awash with examples of entrepreneurs who give away a share of their pie before it's even baked so that everyone around the table can eat further down the line.

Developers actively look for projects that could *be the next big thing* and take equity instead of cash as their method of remuneration. Sounds like tech nirvana right? The entrepreneur isn't out of pocket and the developer could get a percentage of something huge. But is it as easy as that?

Unfortunately, no. Let's start with the DOs, if you're thinking about giving away equity for development.

- Do your due diligence on whomever you decide to work with. A good developer should have plenty of references he can rattle off in a heartbeat.

- Do check out their portfolio of work, see if it works, and try to break it (only kidding…OK we're not kidding).

- Do have an honest discussion about their motivations for working on the project. You might be trying to change the world with revenue being a far second on your list. Conversely, they could be trying to get rich. At some point heads will butt.

- Do have an appreciation of the task ahead. It will mean that if things take twice as long as your Gantt chart says you won't be going grey over it.

- Do have a clear vision of the product that you're building and document this in a way that can be understood by a third party. Having it in your head is helpful to you, but probably just you.

- Do give away enough equity to motivate the developers. There's no point thinking that you negotiated them down to 0.1% for 10 years worth of development work, because at some point the penny will drop that it's not worth the developers' time and they'll go missing in action.

- Do think creatively about how you can give away your equity. Deals that involve part cash part equity are commonplace.

- Do give your development team space to 'get on with it.'

- Do express any concerns you have early on about the direction of the development because undoing a day's work can set the project back more than one day.

And now the DON'Ts!

* Don't just pluck an equity figure out of the sky (if you can help it!). A guestimate is better than a complete guess. It will help you to justify on both sides the equity share further down the line.

* Don't be closed to new ideas and a new direction from the developer(s). Remember that it's now their 'baby' too and they have a vested interest in the project.

* Don't forget to actually draw up a shareholder agreement. As grown up as it sounds, it's better than a handshake over a pint.

* Don't be afraid to pull the plug on the arrangement if it's just not working out. A happy breakup is better than an unhappy marriage.

* Don't be rigid. If it becomes obvious that the project is leaving the scope of what was expected at the start, then offering and renegotiating terms should be the order of the day.

There is a huge element of risk and reward in technology and none more than in the initial equity discussions between the entrepreneur and the developer(s). Don't rush it because it will only come back to bite you in the end.

Good luck and happy negotiating!

When to Go Mobile

The problem we are facing while writing this is that the case for mobile is growing by the day. So we are going to answer this question from 'us' today and the future 'us'.

The answer from the 'us' today is to do both web and mobile at the same time. The answer from the future 'us' is to go mobile first and build web after. We won't bore you with the stats of mobile growing at a zillion %; you can see with our own eyes what's happening.

But going mobile can sometimes mean developing a mobile-specific business and revenue model. This can mean that web considerations are axed or tricky to shoehorn. The answer really depends on your product's value proposition and the problem you're trying to solve. From an investment perspective, rolling out on web and mobile at the same can sometimes be prohibitive.

We can hear some of you asking, "What about a mobile-responsive website?" Well, that can be a solution but remember the real value of a mobile app is in the user experience. A mobile app is only valuable if it can do something a website can't.

Then there's the issue of traction to consider. What platform are your target users more likely to use? If you don't know, *ask them*! Use SurveyMonkey or something, but don't guess this one. It will be far too costly in the mid-term. Then you'll need to consider what your users will do on a mobile phone against what they'll do on the web; or at least how they'll do it. What is the functional priority when they take your phone out of their pocket to do 'x' against when they are on a comfy sofa ready to spend some quality time on their laptop?

All of these considerations make for a zigzag approach to the answer. If you're trying to 'cram it all in,' that just won't work on mobile. Allowing people to perform the headline tasks that your product is built on would take top priority.

Shifting the startup mindset from *going mobile* to *being mobile* from the jump is extremely important. Understanding the mobile context and its relevance to your market is more important. It will not answer 'when you should go mobile' but 'how you should go mobile.'

This is the important question.

Building your revenue model with mobile in mind will help to future-proof your startup and enable you to take a proactive stance and anticipate the direction of the market without having to be on the developmental back foot.

Once you've crossed the mobile development finish line, how will you market your app, keep people coming, and have them evangelize your prized piece of work? Do your best not to become the app statistic that highlights how many apps are used once and eventually get deleted.

On Scaling the Business

What does a US-based entrepreneur see when he opens the door of his garage?
300 million customers.

What does a Finnish entrepreneur see when he opens the door of his garage?
3 meters of snow.

So they say in Finland.
Scaling the business is key to achieving a big exit. Venture-based tech startups

need to scale quickly to grow the valuation of the business rapidly and achieve the desired return multiple for the angel and institutional investors.

US-based startups are lucky to have a huge home market in front of them. But still, sooner or later there will be a time for them to become international. In other parts of the world, entrepreneurs are not that lucky. Their home markets are small and selling abroad becomes a necessity very soon. We have dedicated a separate chapter in the section In Marketing & Sales on discussing when the time is right to go abroad.

Let us for now focus on scaling the business, independently of doing it in the home market or abroad.

Scaling in essence is about customer acquisition, cross- and up-selling, and customer retention. What can be done? We take for granted that the entrepreneur has developed an attractive product that solves a real problem or satisfies a real desire (as discussed in a previous chapter), has successfully managed the technology risk, and has launched a product in the marketplace.

We also have to remember that the company is economically viable only if the customer acquisition cost is lower than the customer lifetime value (see more details in a specific chapter on this subject), and that the company needs to be able to sell and deliver the product in the most cost-effective way. Therefore, customer acquisition and service activation needs to be as much zero-touch as possible to keep the need for human intervention and associated expenses low.

With these two prerequisites in place, the key to customer acquisition is to get the brand and the product known in the marketplace and/or found on the Internet. This is where the entrepreneur has to relentlessly focus. This is not just about SEO and SEM. Just like a big company, the startup has to find and employ the right marketing mix. In this book, we dedicate several chapters to this rather complex subject of marketing and sales to provide some insight, tips, and tricks, but we highly recommend you work with an expert in the field who knows what he is doing.

Customer acquisition is also about putting in place the most effective sales channels. And specific measures to improve conversion need to be incorporated into the marketing plan as well.

Then come cross- and up-selling, and enticing repeat purchases from existing customers. Both are driven by permanent customer engagement and walking the fine line between being too intrusive vs. not engaging sufficiently.

And finally, there is customer retention that is closely related to the exit barriers the business has created. In addition, the product offering needs to be kept fresh and attractive over its lifetime.

To be successful, the startup needs measuring because what you don't measure, you don't control. Metrics are crucial and many investors assess the health and traction of a business by scrutinizing the metrics. The entrepreneur needs to use metrics to assess the effectiveness of his marketing mix and actions and to enable him to maximize the impact of a given marketing budget. The marketing actions breathe life into the company, and the dashboard of metrics is a tool to steer them into the right direction.

Protection of Intellectual Property

Protection of intellectual property (IP) is a topic the entrepreneur needs to work on with a specialized lawyer. The only thing we can offer in this chapter is to give an overview of some basic concepts related to intellectual property and its protection in order to set the stage for a conversation with a professional in the field.

As a basic principle, intellectual property has attached a range of legal rights that may vary by type of property. These types range from confidential information and copyrights to trademarks, patents, and others. Each type is treated differently, and some types can or need to be registered.

Confidential information may include trade secrets, know how, or assets that are not capable of statutory IP protection. Confidential information, however, needs to be marked as confidential to be able to be protected.
Copyrights are used to identify the creator of an intellectual property to allow the creator to control the use of the copyrighted material. Copyright protection is automatic.

Trademarks can be unregistered or registered, are often used for trade names and logos, and can be marked with the 'TM' or ® symbol respectively.
Patents grant an inventor the exclusive right to use the invention and are related to the functional and technical aspects of the invention. Patents need to be registered.

Registration is in general limited to certain territories. The entrepreneur needs to be aware of the territorial limitations and register the IP in the territories of his interest and economic activity.

Unfortunately, intellectual property law is complicated and not fully unified across borders, and despite its importance it is often considered as something intangible and negligible. Some entrepreneurs might consider registration expensive. Many entrepreneurs unfortunately don't pay enough attention.

The only advice we can give here to the entrepreneur is to take IP protection very seriously and work with an expert in the field.

TWO

On Marketing and Sales

On Market Risk
(Revisited)

It comes as no surprise that many startups fail, given the disproportionate risk of their business. That level of risk is the fundamental reason why seed and early-stage investors require hefty risk premiums to compensate for those portfolio companies that face an involuntary exit (AKA go bust) or produce only meager returns.

But what is the risk really? There are two types: technology risk and market risk. Each type needs to be mitigated differently.

Technology risk is basically the probability that the technology being developed does not work as expected. Some technologies face huge technology risk. This is particularly the case when development cycles are long and costly and official approvals by the authorities are required before the technology is allowed to be commercialized. Nano- and biotechnologies typically fall into this category. Take cancer treatment for instance. It takes years from initial lab research though testing and approval before the technology can hit the market. Once it is on the market, however, the potential for market success is enormous, for obvious reasons. You can find more on technology risk in a previous chapter.

For software and Internet technologies, the technology risk should not be denied, however the major risk factor is market risk. Will clients buy the software? Will users find the new eCommerce site, and once found, will they convert into buying customers? Will the technology be able to sustain initial growth, and for how long? Will clients abroad adopt the technology the same way as the technology's home market, and which changes need to be made to assure global adoption? How will competitors react on your market launch and what measures will they take to retaliate? Will new competitors emerge and eat into your market share in a market that might even have been created by you? This is a particularly important concern with technologies that rely on intellectual property that is difficult to protect. How easy or difficult is it for your competitors to copy your technology and offer something similar, or even better? This might actually be an easy task for them now that you have climbed up the learning curve and a new market has been built by you spending your money. They have saved that money and now might be better funded than you, thus they can spend more on marketing and sales and eventually outperform you in the marketplace. Or they might be able to offer a more attractive price than you.

These are some of the questions startups are facing. And investors will scrutinize your responses to them. Their willingness to invest will depend by and large on your plan to address these risks, its credibility and feasibility, and your ability to execute it.

So what is it you need to do?

First, you need to put yourself in the shoes of your customers and try to figure out why they would want to adopt your technology or what would hold them back from adopting it. In other words, figure out potential barriers to adoption. This is not a theoretical exercise and your opinion or gut feeling count little in the brutal world of a free market. It's the customer who matters and decides what to buy and who to buy it from, and you need to engage with him as early as possible, and do so in the field away from your desk.

Questions you have to come to grips with include:

- How do I get found?
- How do people hear about me?
- How do customers buy my product?
- What are they really looking for?
- Why would they buy my technology in the first place?
- Why would they prefer my technology to my competitors'?
- What would hold them up from buying my technology?

Second, once you have gained some market traction, you need to ask yourself:

- How can I address a broader market?
- How can I entice repeat purchases?
- How can I increase the stickiness of my product?
- How can I increase loyalty and customer retention?
- How can I avoid customer churn-off to competitors?
- What barriers of entry do I have to create for my current and future competitors?

And a final consideration: when and how to expand abroad? You will find more about this important topic in a later chapter.

Pitching and Selling Your Idea

Early on in the development of your idea, be it conceptually or technically, you'll need to be prepared to pitch and sell that idea.

Some of our considerations in other parts of the book included getting developers onboard for equity, raising investment, and building a team. Unless you can get people onboard, then this is going to be a struggle. Now don't worry; you don't have to be the most charismatic or even dynamic person in the world to pitch or sell your idea. It simply requires the ability to communicate your vision and the reason why your tech idea is the best.

One of the easiest ways to get your idea across today is through the use of storytelling. Chances are, the problem you're trying to solve or the value you're trying to add to your users may have a scenario. Take Shazam, for example. How many times have you heard a song on the radio or in the club and wondered "Who sung that?" Well, Shazam, as we're sure you're aware, solves that problem.

What's your users' scenario? Or in tech speak use case? Once you can distill this down to a sentence or two, then you have the beginnings of an elevator pitch. The elevator pitch is an essential part of your startup arsenal. It's something you need to be able to pull out like an old Western gunslinger.

But the purpose of the elevator pitch isn't necessarily to convert anyone; it's to grab the attention of your audience. Be that a developer at the start of a hackathon or a potential investor at a networking event.

Once you've got their attention, you need to have a very well-prepared pitch long
enough to convert. This must not be War and Peace but concise and to the point.

1. Start by telling a story, providing the use case for your technology.
2. Explain how you intend to solve that problem.
3. Discuss how you'll build the solution.
4. Talk about how you'll attract your audience.
5. Explain how you'll keep your audience.
6. Discuss your revenue model.
7. Talk about your competitors and what makes you different.
8. Show an appreciation for how you will future-proof the model.
9. Let whomever you're pitching to know what it is you want from them and how they'll benefit, be that an investor with a return, or a developer with an upside, etc.

When pitching today, less is more. It's not about having a ton of bullet points on your presentation, but enough so that you can carry on the narrative in a more conversational way rather than beating your audience over the head with PowerPoint.

The last thing to remember when pitching and selling your idea is that you've got to believe in it 120%. Your passion and enthusiasm will not only be contagious but it will be an essential part of keeping everyone involved motivated and onside.

How to Target Your Audience, Create Share of Mind and Convert It into Sales

Many companies launch Internet businesses in a quest for claiming their share in this ever-growing market. Growth rates clearly indicate that there are plenty of sizable business opportunities that are just waiting out there to be capitalized on. On the other hand, we also see many Internet businesses faltering.

In the technology sector, something similar is happening. Many young companies spend six-figure amounts on developing leading-edge technology solutions destined to change to the world, just to find that nobody seems to want them. Some even receive grants from governmental organizations, win startup competitions, and receive R&D tax credits. Others spin out from universities through the universities' technology transfer offices, after years of sophisticated research activity. Still, market success is not guaranteed.

Let us face the facts. The nicest piece of technology is worth little unless it gains significant market traction. And investors are generally more interested in the plans to take a certain technology to market than in the technology itself.

The first and foremost challenge each startup is up against therefore is how to get known in the marketplace and attract the attention of potential buyers. Getting found on the Internet is often the biggest problem for a young and small company, given the lack of resources to afford extensive marketing campaigns.

When asking entrepreneurs about their products' competitive advantage, they often claim the superiority of their functionality and usability compared to all their competitors' offerings. But does that really matter?

It does, but only to a certain extent. Obviously, nobody will buy a product that offers a poor functionality and is painful to use. Well, that's not 100% true; some people even by those products. However, how will customers realize that there is a superior product out there unless they can easily find it? That is the key. There are so many websites on the Internet, applications on the various application stores, and technologies that sound alike and serve similar purposes, that getting found is a huge challenge. To make things worse, many technology businesses – as one would expect – are being founded by entrepreneurs with a technology background, not necessarily with a marketing background. But they shouldn't be blind to the need for professional marketing experts.

'Build it and they will come' will work only in very specific circumstances, as we have seen in a previous chapter. Success in the technology business therefore needs to be built on a balanced mix of technology and marketing & sales skills, and that mix also needs to be reflected in the use of available funding.

Some entrepreneurs argue that they need to focus on technology development first, before spending any time, effort, and money on marketing. Although this sounds somewhat logical, this view often leads to failure. The approach of the 'lean startup' – originally developed by Eric Ries and published in his bestselling book *The Lean Startup* – 'minimum viable product' (abbreviated MVP) and 'pivoting' is basically about hitting the ground as early as possible to get real customers use your product and provide feedback rapidly. It allows you to pivot and adjust direction early on to meet the real needs of your customers, not the needs you might have thought were real. Staying in a lab environment too long won't give you that opportunity.

And more importantly, investors want to see market traction before committing any investment money. What does that mean for you? It means that this becomes a battle for the share of mind of your customers of which you have to win your fair share and convert it into sales. How are you going to do that?

First, start your marketing effort as soon as you possibly can.

Second, target your marketing wisely towards your marketing goals to create awareness and interest first, then desire and action to buy (the AIDA principle).

Third, use a balanced mix of inbound and outbound marketing. Inbound marketing has become popular recently as an alternative to the more classical outbound marketing approach. It is more cost effective and less intrusive and adapts better to focused awareness campaigns on a very specific technology. It is all about getting people to know you, your brand, and your product by publishing content that is relevant to them, thus creating your fair share in their mind. Once you have mind share, market share will follow. There is an abundance of literature and experts on inbound marketing who you can resort to. And we have dedicated several chapters to this important topic.

And finally, DIY is a no-no. Nobody is perfect in everything, and many entrepreneurs are great in developing new technologies. Marketing is too important to leave it in the hands of first-timers, amateurs, and wannabe professionals. It is highly advisable that you complement your team with real experts in the field of marketing of new technologies who have a proven track record of successful product marketing despite having been forced to working with limited budgets.

On Customer Acquisition Cost

Many young companies bank their business model on significant growth, in line with Internet and eCommerce, as well as smartphone growth rates we see today. They quote studies on the number of smartphones that will exist on the planet by 201X, and the fact that in a few years' time the number of smartphones will have surpassed the population on earth. Thus, they argue that the market they can address is huge.

Others quote statistics that show the rise of Internet sales to the detriment of High Street to justify the size of their market opportunity for their brand new eCommerce site. Still others point to the fact that for their specific product, sales through the web is lagging behind the average and that therefore an enormous market is still up for grabs.

That might all be true. However, whilst analyzing smartphone market numbers is crucial for smartphone vendors, for a developer of smartphone applications it is at best a proxy and just gives some vague idea of market potential.

So why bother with these numbers anyways? When building an investment case, a mature company can rely on more or less accurate historic numbers on market size, growth, and their own market share. Based on these facts, those companies can project with certain precision their future revenue opportunity. After all, they are often just looking for improvement rather than disruptive innovation (see the chapter on product innovation 101 for more details).

For young companies, in particular for those that sell emerging technology, these data are simply not available. Therefore, a business case needs to be built bottom-up based on two parameters: Customer acquisition cost (abbreviated CAC) and customer lifetime value (CLV). Investors look at these numbers together with growth rates, to project future revenues and profits.

Customer acquisition cost is defined in Wikipedia as "the resource a business needs to allocate in order to acquire an additional customer." There is also the customer retention cost (abbreviated CRC), the amount of money to be spent to retain an existing customer, i.e. to prevent him from going to the competition.

How are these being measured? In a mass-market marketing campaign, you need to think about how big the audience is you will reach with your campaign and how many of your visitors you will convert into buying customers. Customer acquisition cost therefore is measured as the sum of the total costs of the campaign, including associated overhead, divided by the number of converted customers gained through that campaign.

In a channel sales situation, you basically need to calculate the cost of the channel, including sales commissions and overhead, you need to incur to acquire a new customer. And in direct sales, it is the fully-loaded cost of your sales force and their sales initiatives and efforts required to win a new customer.

These are all upfront costs that need to be compensated by the customer lifetime value (abbreviated CLV). Wikipedia defines customer lifetime value as "a prediction of the net profit attributed to the entire future relationship with a customer." An alternative definition given is "the dollar value of a customer relationship, based on the present value of the projected future cash flows from the customer relationship."

The key now is to find the right balance of CAC and CLV. If you spend little on CAC, you might (or might not) be able to win a few very valuable clients at a very low cost (early adopters for instance). However, your total number of customers won't grow fast and big enough to get investors excited.

If, on the other hand, you spend a high amount on CAC, you will certainly win customers with high CLV, but also many with a CLV that is so low that it will hardly or never compensate the CAC, following *the law of diminishing returns* (also called *the law of increasing relative cost*).

How to find that balance is easier said than done. When you start, you will need to do some modeling and simulation. You should get statistics and comparisons with similar businesses, and above all resort to an expert in the field, to someone who has done it before. During ongoing operations, it is about measuring, measuring, and measuring: measuring the impact of each sales campaign you undertake, on a permanent basis.

What Are Your Routes to Market?

'Build it and they will come.' We have seen already in a previous chapter that more than often it doesn't work like this. To be successful in sales, the company needs to choose its routes to market wisely.

"We are a business partner of corporation X and Y." That's what entrepreneurs often tell us. But how much top-line revenue do these partnerships really generate?

"I will spend 50% of my funding on online and social marketing." Of course you will. A young company will certainly not spend huge amounts on TV ads. That's obvious. But how are you going to maximize the impact of your online and social marketing?

"I use SEO/SEM and SMO to get market traction." That's right, that's what you do. But everyone else does the same. So how do you stand out from the pack?

"I sell direct to blue chip companies." A good idea, but will they buy from you given that they are large and you are small? What is the size of the sales force you need to meet your sales projections? And can you remunerate your sales representatives competitively so that they want to work for you and not for others, others including large and mature companies with massive brand recognition where selling and making sales quotas is so much easier?

"I outsource my sales activities to agents, specialized outsourced sales providers, and individual business developers." That's not a bad idea either, but do you reward them sufficiently so that they go the extra mile for you?

There are a lot of questions, but what are the answers? Let's start with the investor's view. "Sales Cure All" is a quote attributed to Mark Cuban. "Know how your company will make money and how it will actually make sales." As we will see in later chapters, investors look for a significant return at the point of exit, and the valuation at the exit largely depends on the revenue and EBITDA of the company.

That's why venture capitalists in general want to see real market traction before making any investment. You need to demonstrate that traction through real sales success, through metrics when you sell to the consumer market, and through closed sales and a sales pipeline when you sell to business customers. And to generate these sales, you need routes to market. So what are they?

First and foremost, you need to understand how people buy, which determines the routes you need to take to sell to them. Here are some examples:

Consumers increasingly buy through the Internet. However, High Street is not dead and plays a crucial role in supplying goods to certain consumer segments. We also find that some people search for products on the Internet and buy them in a physical store, whilst others do exactly the opposite, checking products out (the touch, feel, look, size) on High Street and then buy them online. Obviously, in a business that needs to grow fast, you need to sell through the Internet, but there are also scalable technologies that enable merchants (with physical retail outlets) to sell through the Internet, accept and process credit and debit card payments, manage customer loyalty, etc.

The AIDA principle has been used for decades to model the pre-sales cycle: attention (awareness), interest, desire, action. Figure out how it works for you, how you get found by potential customers, how to attract their attention and create interest in your products and the desire to buy them, and how to make customers act, i.e. make them actually buy your products, thus convert them into paying customers. How to retain them and entice repeat purchases is your next battlefield.

When selling to businesses, things are quite different. Again, ask yourself how the AIDA principle applies to your company. But more importantly, find out how and from whom your target clients buy. There are established distribution channels to serve certain markets, be it value-added resellers, system integrators, strategic technology partners, or others. Many corporations and small- and medium-size companies buy from these channels only, they know them, they trust them, they are used to interacting with them without major frictions, and they often have certified them and have established framework or master service agreements. You need to identify them and use them to your advantage, and theirs – in a win-win relationship.

You'll find more details on how to do this in the following chapters.

SEO/SEM and Google Marketing Tips and Tricks

In case you were wondering, Google isn't going anywhere in spite of the heavy social network activity that has changed how we use the Internet. Google still remains the #1 place to find out about stuff and is an extremely valuable marketing tool for any tech startup in need of traffic to their sign-up page.

Whole books have been written on the topics of search engine optimization (SEO) and search engine marketing (SEM or pay-per-click). But below we'd like to bring to the surface some of the overarching considerations when attempting your foray into either.

SEO Tips and Tricks

1. Firstly, and it's a roundabout way to make the point, but whenever you see the two words SEO and 'trick' in the same sentence, run for the hills. Google has a whole department called the "Web Spam Team" headed by a fellow called Matt Cutts who spend their life ensuring that Google cannot be 'tricked'.

2. SEO is no longer a dark art. Google has an extremely useful webmaster YouTube channel where you can get lots of 'tips' on how to make Google love your website.

3. As we speak, Google has introduced 'social signals' into its ranking algorithm. This means that (genuine) likes and followers will help Google determine how great you are as a brand.

4. Google, if you think about it, simply hyperlinks to content. It's the king of content. With that said, it knows if people are engaged with your content by tracking how long they stay on the page, if they check out the rest of your site and if they share it with their network. So create great content that will hold your audiences attention until they eventually do something you really want them to like: download your new tech!

5. Think multimedia. The next time you view a Google results page, you'll notice that there are no longer just drab blue links with text underneath. Google has included video, images, and maps to its search results pages. What does this tell you? Well, get some video, images (and if appropriate), maps! The more types of content you create to engage your audience, the better Google will rate you.

SEM Tips and Tricks

1. Be different. We don't really read a Google results page, we skim it. We look for keywords and phrases that we feel speak to us and will find us what we're looking for. With that in mind, consider what will grab your audience's attention and do that!

2. The click promise. Google will reward you if after someone clicks on your advert they take action and don't immediately click back to another result. It tells Google that whatever you've said in your advert must be true because people

3. Test, test, and test again. Google pay-per-click costs money, so you want to make sure you're getting a return on your marketing dollars. The easiest way to do this is to test the ads that work and get rid of the ones that don't.

4. Speak to Google! They used to be hidden away out of the reach for mere mortals like us, but today you can call a Google rep and have him help you with the setup of your Adwords campaign. How great is that?

5. Have a budget. Google, as much as we love them, will happily take your cash and run. OK they won't run but you get the gist. It's not their business, it's yours. So have a strict budget that you're happy to experiment with in the short term until it starts working for you.

It is worth noting that using SEO and SEM in conjunction is a useful strategy. In an ideal world you'll have enough cash and resources to do both, and if you do then here's a suggestion for you: If you're targeting 50 keywords using SEM, then in tandem focus on a bunch of those keywords, say 20 of them, with your SEO efforts. As soon as they start appearing on the front page of Google in the natural listings, then you can stop paying for them in the paid listings.

The 10 Secrets of Social Media Marketing

We are going to make the assumption that by virtue of the fact that you're considering starting up a technology startup, you're pretty *au fait* with social media. However, we are not going to assume that just because you know how to Tweet about breakfast that you're a dab hand at marketing through social media.

So let's go through what we like to call the "10 Secrets..." or ideas if you will that will help kick-start your success story on social media.

Secret number 1: *How to build powerful customers relationships using social media*

One word: Engagement! The thing to remember is that when two people get engaged there's a commitment that takes place on both sides. Your audience commit to interacting with you providing you commit to delivering something engaging for them to interact with. This could be a blog, a video, a game, infographics, or whatever. Lastly, remember that commitment is usually a long-term thing, more of a marathon than a sprint. So get your running shoes on!

Secret number 2: *Get complete strangers to evangelize your products or services*

We like to tell people about great products or services because we like the kudos of being the person who has delivered some value into other people's lives. But we also like to 'big up' our friends and people who we feel a natural affinity to. This is where you, Mr./Mrs. Tech Startup can make an easy win. Industry-dependent of course, be friendly, warm, funny, smart, witty, and other adjectives you know will resonate with your target. This has nothing to do with your actual product offering but more to do with how you're packaging it.

Secret number 3: Get personal!

People can sometimes be apologetic about their aspirations, the people they want to help, the world they want to change, the software they want to develop, and the big problem they want to solve for a few. Everyone has a story and a reason why they're doing what they're doing. The problem is that it's oftentimes not shared or used as leverage for the task at hand. We feel that those things are too close to our chest, too personal, and not business-y enough. If you're the big corporation or have just had VC backing then you can maybe just throw enough marketing money at the problem until it goes away. But if you're that small business or boot-strapped entrepreneur you need to create a buzz sooner rather than later. Without theorizing too much, here are some examples to bring some clarity to this secret.

Secret number 4: Why working backwards is the best way to go

Knowing where you want your business to be in one year, three years, or five years from now is key to understanding why this secret is so important. Let's use a mathematical example based on a revenue target, say generating $100k in
year 1.

The Objective

- Company target - $100k in revenues in year 1.
- Company product/service average unit price - $200.
- To make $100k, the company would have to sell 500 units.
- This equals 41 units per month or 10 units per week.

How to Achieve This?

Over a 6-month period the company calculates:

- For every 50 followers it gains on Twitter who engage with them, 3 customers convert to their website.
- For every 50 fans on Facebook who engage with them, they get 5 more customers convert to their website.
- Based on this alone, it would mean that over the year they would have to get 4.000 Twitter followers and 2.500 Facebook fans.

Secret number 5: *The biggest social media mistake and how to avoid it*

Don't control the conversation. Thomas Power of leadORS says that traditional companies are CSC, or closed, selective and controlling. However, in the digital world in order respond to the modern day, one has to be ORS, which is open, random and supportive.

Most companies try to control the conversation that happens on social media; they are selective with whom they interact, and they close off scenarios which take them out of their comfort zone.

Avoid these at all cost.

Secret number 6: *Increase your productivity tenfold using social media*

Simple. Leverage technology! It's there for a reason, so be it Hootsuite, Tweetdeck, or the plethora of tools that exist out there; make good use of them! There's a split camp between automating your social media activity or not. In my opinion, you should automate marketing messages and spend time engaging with your audience in a real way.

Secret number 7: *The one and only number you need when marketing online*

Conversion rate! This is defined as the ratio of visitors who convert casual content views or website visits into desired actions.

Once you know what that conversion rate is, you can then calculate how much money it will take to achieve and thus your overall return on investment. So for example, if you know it costs you $250 (in time, manpower, etc.) to get 500 people to your fan page on Facebook, of which 50 convert and have an average spend of $30, that would equate to a return of $1500 and a profit of $1250.

Secret number 8: *How your story can create a huge buzz*

Everyone loves a story, so give 'em one! You might think, "My story is nothing to write home about!" but you're probably wrong. What you have to remember is that your story is going to, without a doubt, resonate with someone. That person will share your story and it will resonate with someone they know and so on and so forth.

Get the picture? If you're still in doubt then ask a PR professional to help you craft what may seem a dull as dishwater story into something grabby!

Secret number 9: *How to quickly become a thought leader in your industry*

This is central to secret #8 and the reason why you're creating this bit of tech. If you've not watched the video by Simon Sinek on *Start With Why*, then feel free to put down this book and check it out.

OK, you're back. Getting this bit right could catapult you into thought leadership. In real terms, we're talking about the way in which you communicate your innovation.

Secret number 10: *Keeping up with the Joneses*

As we write this book, a new social media platform somewhere is being born. It's probably a losing battle to try and jump on each and every platform that pops up. This is directly related to the resource you have to throw at the marketing of your project.

The key to success here is to create impact on whatever platform you choose to spend your time on, be it Twitter, Facebook, LinkedIn, or Google+. Really invest your time into at least one platform if that's all you have time for. Once you're on top of that one, then move onto the next.

Inbound vs. Outbound and Guerilla Marketing That Works

There is a lot of talk about inbound marketing as the new way vs. the more traditional outbound marketing. But what is really behind both, and which one should be used in a given situation?

Inbound Marketing

The many and varied definitions of inbound marketing are enough to confuse the best of us. Hence, we are taking the liberty of quoting Dr. Paul Bain's tweet (@pmbaintx), *"Meeting prospects WHEN they want, WHERE they want, WHAT they want."* This is perhaps the most simplified understanding of what inbound marketing is all about.

Outbound Marketing

Outbound marketing is the traditional means of marketing. It includes a direct approach to advertising and marketing. With the emergence of the digital marketing era, one would think that outbound marketing has become a dying art, but think again. It is not only marketing budget friendly, but creates a stronger impact on your potential consumers because you are able to interact with them. If someone claims that outbound marketing is dying, clearly point out to the number of emailers in their inbox. Or better yet, point out that the prize money of reality shows are on the rise, led by the demand for advertising space during commercial breaks.

Inbound Marketing vs. Outbound Marketing

Inbound marketing has always seemed to be a more preferable way of marketing because you know where to start. It starts with potential customers and the people who would require your offerings. But then, when you are doing so, you are dealing with more competition as well. Let us just say that your tech startup has a product: online trading software. You know that you have huge potential among Internet users who trade online. So you start an inbound Internet marketing campaign with search engine optimization, blogging, and social media. Start with the keyword 'online trading software'! Imagine all the people that you will be competing against – all of them.

So your SEO marketing should be such that it is able to stand out amongst millions of others. For that, you would need a higher budget for marketing to make sure that the SEO professionals that you are hiring are simply the best. In short, you pay more to stand out in the crowd with inbound marketing. Therefore, inbound marketing is a cost-effective method in niche markets where you compete only with a few other players.

In the case of outbound marketing, however, things are slightly different. You are risking it on an unknown group of people, but this is your potential target audience. The few that are in fact your localized target audience will singularly give you all the attention. Moreover, outbound marketing campaigns have a lower budget. However, outbound marketing or guerilla marketing may also fail if not implemented well. We believe that farsightedness and weighing your risks in choosing your marketing style is the key. But we may not be able to predict it right every time, just as we cannot predict the stock market flawlessly.

Hence, a mix of both inbound and outbound marketing could be the preferable option. Once you are able to grab attention for your tech product with outbound marketing, you can move on to inbound marketing. Successful inbound marketing strategies are those that keep your customer coming back to you and help build brand loyalty.

Guerilla Marketing

Guerrilla Marketing is all about taking the potential consumers by surprise. The surprise factor also helps to create a lasting impression overall. This form of marketing is desirable, as it is said to offer chances of higher ROI. It is understood that for a tech startup, going creative with a serious tech product might be a challenge. However, that is the beauty of guerilla marketing. It can be implemented for any product, as long as you know how to relate it to what you wish to sell. From flash mobs at a train station to a teaser ad in the form of an emailer, anything could prove to be a marketing strategy that works.

On Freemium Models

According to Freemium.org,

"The term freemium is coined using two powerful words 'Free' and 'Premium'. It describes a business model where in you give away a core product for free and then generate revenue by selling premium products to a small percentage of free users ..."

To be clear, the freemium model isn't about giving away a free chapter of a book and then selling the book. It's about giving people something they really want and is actually useful. That's the win for the consumer. The win for the business is that the freemium model is a powerful way to sell the premium version of your widget.

The model of example of a successful freemium model is Skype. They provide a free product used by over 1 billion people and sell additional services on top. Only about 8% of Skype's users actually buy anything, but given the volume of people that use the service, 8% is a sizeable number. Besides, the 92% of people who haven't bought anything are a captive audience that Skype could possibly convert during their life as a user.

So the $64,000 question is: Should you employ the freemium model for your tech?

The answer is very much hinged on your product and the business model. For example, just because you're giving it away for free in the hope people upgrade to a paid service doesn't mean that the free product can be substandard. You'll still need to provide updates, bug fixes, and support. This will probably come at a cost, freemium or premium.

A few of the major pitfalls faced by freemium products are creating a 'nice to have' bit of tech that people like but are never going to pay for. Following this is the investor hot potato. It's true that there are investors who'll throw cash at a freemium idea that has thousands of users but no revenue. This is generally in the hope, however, that it can be sold onto another investor up the line who can throw enough marketing money at it to then monetize.

At this point there's a lot of risk involved because this is far from an exact science and relies on this: If you have a good freemium product then you must have an excellent premium product. "Piece of cake!" we hear you cry, but if you get it wrong and the investor is stuck with the hot potato with no revenue, then guess what? You'll get dropped.

So should you go freemium? Maybe, but focus on mass and even though you'll probably make some sensible assumptions about your revenues, it's essential that you keep your finger firmly on the pulse of your user base. This way, you'll be able to do a trendy pivot when necessary. In this regard, you're taking a proactive rather than reactive approach and the months you'll save could be the difference between success or shut up shop failure.

Secrets of the Up-Sell

Have you ever been offered an upgrade on your flight ticket from economy class to business class by paying a *little extra*? Or, have you been asked to upgrade your burger and Pepsi into a meal at one of the popular burger outlets, with french fries included in the package? Sure, you have, at least the latter one. This is what *up-selling* is all about in its simplest form. This strategy can also be used for your products in a tech startup.

Then there is *cross-selling*, a concept often confused with *up-selling*. Upgrading leads is up-selling, while simple add-ons at a little cost is termed as cross-selling. Remember the last time you ordered a pizza and they suggested that you pay a little extra for a drink to go with it? That's when you have been cross-sold to.

Tricks can Make Up-Selling a Cake Walk – with Extra Icing

So how do you use the up-selling strategy for your tech startup? The secrets don't lie in some treasure chest locked and lost in time, but simply with the customers themselves.

- *Address what the customer wants.* The customer is not looking for what you think is good for him, but what he thinks is good for him. So if he is choosing a package that he wants, do not force on him things that he doesn't. Try to find out what his purpose ultimately is when he chooses a particular product. Second, find out his preferences. Once you have or your staff has practiced selling, experience would teach you how to drive up-selling on account of what your potential customer wants.

- *Pointing out the benefits.* When the customer chooses a package from you and wishes to upgrade the package, make sure that the benefits are clearly stated. Here is the key: Explain the benefits that specifically serve his purpose. Show him how his purpose will be served better with the upgrade. This is easier with technology products because you can up-sell efficiency and quality, beyond giving the customer the benefit of just giving him more of the same.

- *Convenience products strategically placed for impulse buys.* This is simply the idea conveyed when you say, "Would you like some fries with that?" Customers don't want more unless you make them realize that they might want more.

- *Close the deal quickly (but don't get greedy).* If your customer has agreed quickly to an upgrade, avoid trying to upgrade the package further. This might lead you to lose the customer laying the golden egg before you can say, "See you soon." A lot of people believe up-selling is a trick, so if a customer has agreed to the up-sell, he is already building a relationship with you. Try not to destroy it.

- *Do not blatantly up-sell.* There are ways to subtly up-sell. Make it look like you are just informing the customer about another product that he can try. A lot of sales people lose customers by talking too much about it. Instead, show him the product on a brochure or through an email. Let him be the judge and make him feel that he has chosen it for himself eventually without having been influenced by you to buy it.

Consumers today are more educated than you might imagine. In the field of technology, they are in fact as smart as you are, so subtly being smart about a sale is the best way to make up-selling work. Also note that existing customers are easier to up-sell to. Don't up-sell to a consumer who is in doubt about choosing your package in the first place.

When to Go Abroad

"I'd like to go to Silicon Valley as soon as possible," so many startups outside the US say. And within the US, many want to follow the example of Facebook to go to Silicon Valley first, and then expand internationally into Europe and the rest of the world.

There is nothing wrong with these aspirations. But what does 'as soon as possible' really mean? When is the right time?

Some non-US entrepreneurs argue the sooner the better, because they would like to start penetrating the highly advanced and by far largest market for new technologies as soon as they possibly can. US-based startups like to follow the success of Facebook and settle in Silicon Valley to become part of the most vibrant and mature entrepreneurial ecosystem in the world. Given the sheer size of their domestic market, they often see expanding overseas as second priority.

This brings up some interesting questions: Why do startups really want to move to a new location? There are many equally valid reasons:

* Access to markets
* Access to talent
* Costs
* Access to funding
* Tax schemes and rates

Let us explore these one at a time.

Access to markets: For many technologies, client proximity is key to sales success. This is particularly true for enterprise products, which often require time-consuming consultative sales efforts with a lot of personal client interactions. Despite the increased popularity of video and conference calls, you simply cannot beat personal relationships and contacts. Therefore, having a sales representative in select target markets is a smart thing.

You have several options: Send someone from your home country, hire someone abroad, or use external business development executives, distributors or an outsourced sales force. In large and far-away markets, it might well be advisable to locate part of the management team there. Many non-US companies do that in the US.

Internet-based businesses, mainly consumer businesses, will say that location doesn't really matter. But it does. First of all, consumer behavior, tastes, and preferences are different in each country and you need to get a solid understanding of these in each country you serve in order to be successful. You need to be immersed in the local culture to get a real grasp of the peculiarities in each market, at least in the larger markets you serve.

Access to talent is equally important and closely related to **costs**. You can probably find talented professionals in most parts of the world, at different levels of quality and costs. But you need top-notch developers and marketing, sales, and management talent, which some entrepreneurs believe you can find mostly in the US. There is also the phenomenon of clusters that should not be underestimated. Talent attracts talent, and talent accepts higher costs of living just to be part of the cluster. That's why it might be beneficial to you to establish your company within a cluster for your specific technology. An additional advantage is that clusters, due to their specialization, offer an easy way for clients to source innovative solutions from startups, which in turn opens up better sales opportunities for your company.

On **access to funding**, there are many statistics that show that the availability and spend of venture capital varies enormously between countries. As we explain in later chapters, seed and early-stage investors tend to invest in companies only in their proximity or at least within their local legislation. Therefore, setting up the company's head office closer to key investors is often required.

Finally, **tax schemes and rates** vary significantly from country and country, as do tax advantages for entrepreneurs and investors. There are many tax schemes including R&D tax credits, tax reliefs for entrepreneurs, tax schemes for investors (e.g. tax relief in case of losses), and many others. There are also governmental grants, startup loans, and funding matching schemes available in some countries. These advantages as a whole can significantly increase or diminish the attractiveness of a specific location or country.

One more consideration: Don't forget the exit. The by-far largest exit market for technology startups is the US, for both IPO and trade sale. Therefore, it is crucial for most non-US startups to establish a presence in the US when the time is right.

THREE

On Funding and
Fundraising

What Investors Are Really Looking for

What are investors really looking for? This is a cardinal question. Some people argue that investors are looking for innovative products and top-of-mind technologies with the potential for exponential growth. Others say that investors invest above all in the team, in great people with a vision and able to pivot rapidly at any sign of adversity to turn their vision into reality.

There is certainly some truth in each of these points. Obviously, nobody wants to invest into me-too products with limited market potential, or in companies with a leadership team that doesn't get anything done. But things are not that easy.

Many investors have a simple answer to this cardinal question. They want three things: exit, exit, and exit. And that is very true. Think about it! Somebody is willing to give his own money or the money of his limited partners to you and have it locked away for many years to come with no liquidity at all in a company where he has only a minority share, truly limiting his influence on decision making. He's willing to invest in a company that is developing something that nobody has done before, selling it in a market that still has to be made, with a competitive landscape that is still to develop, moving in uncharted territory, starting out from nothing on a shoestring budget with a tiny team. That is what venture investing is about.

So what do these high-risk investors want to get in return? A significant return-multiple on their initial investment, often 10x or more. Why a multiple that high? It's very simple: because smart investors invest in a portfolio of companies, with many that fail, and others just returning the investment with no upside. And investors need the exit-as-liquidity event to get their return, given there is only a small secondary market for private non-listed companies. It is as simple as that.

Professional investors view each investment on its own merits. And they will look for:

- Technologies they can understand and that solve real problems.
- Businesses that have the potential for exponential growth, can easily scale internationally, and have founders with the intention to do so (not 'lifestyle businesses').
- Products that are sufficiently differentiated and enjoy if possible a first-mover advantage.
- A sales-driven manage ment team.
- A marketing and sales strategy and plan that assures fast market adoption and growth.

- A clear understanding of market segmentation and routes to market that are being or will be used to gain market reach in a cost-effective way.
- A street-smart, well-balanced team with a bias for action that can make things happen.
- Company founders who the investor would like to work with.
- Financial projections that allow him to achieve the expected return.

To address return expectations, we highly recommend devising a funding roadmap from the current round through to exit, to show a reasonable estimate of follow-on funding requirements to grow the business, to deliver the numbers in the business case and to achieve the desired return.

In addition, we suggest you to be very clear about the use of funds, a break down in categories like product development, marketing and sales, working capital requirements, etc. A classification using accounting terms like salaries makes little sense, as it doesn't show what these salaries are really used for. The focus must be always on revenue-generating activities. Non-revenue-generating expenses need to be kept to a bare minimum.

How to Get Investment Pre and Post-Revenue

"Company X has closed a Series A round of funding of $4m despite not having generated any revenues yet." This is what we hear entrepreneurs telling us time and again and this specific case might be actually true. There are many others, but it makes absolutely no sense picking one case or another to make a point. Each case is different. What you need to look at are patterns — patterns that startups and investors typically follow.

Experience shows that being post-revenue vs. pre-revenue makes a huge difference. It is a step change. Pre-revenue companies basically are still going through a 'theoretical exercise'. They have no real-world proof points for their business case. They might have a real minimum viable product (MVP), but market adoption is still to be seen. Regardless, plans always change when the rubber hits the road.

Having paying customers (and we mean customers, not a single customer and paying customers, not beta testers) gives a first indication of market traction. Real customers willing to pay for the product the price you ask for are key. It also gives an indication that your chosen sales channels are producing first results. That is the step change we are talking about.

What does that mean for fundraising? Again, there are few written rules. To get a better understanding, you need to look at the investor's expectations (see previous chapter). There are basically angel investors (sometimes also called business angels) who invest their own money, often in a syndicate with others. And then there are venture capital firms (VCs) who invest the money of their funds. The major differences are the stage of investment and the size of the investment, as well as the risk the investor is willing to assume and the related return he expects.

As a rule of thumb, when you are pre-revenue, angel investors are a common source of funding. They typically invest locally and funding sizes vary from country to country. The wealth of individuals and the size of the local market where the startup needs to gain initial traction are different in each country, with a huge difference between the US and even the largest European countries. That explains in part why funding rounds in general are bigger in the US than in European or other countries. The reason for angel investors investing locally is their desire to be in close proximity to a high-risk investment. Also, they don't want to complicate their lives with international investments and their related terms. These are good, solid reasons.

When you are post-revenue and can demonstrate initial or even better significant market traction, then VCs are a good source of funding. There are early-stage and growth-stage VCs and some larger firms cover both. Early-stage VCs in general also look for opportunities in proximity to their home country and don't shop around on a worldwide scale. And there is a clear concentration of VCs in certain geographic regions or countries.

Both types of investors have one thing in common. They judge an investment opportunity on a set of criteria:

- The market and its size and growth potential.
- The product or technology, the problem it solves or desire it satisfies, and the level of its differentiation vis-à-vis its competitors.
- The marketing & sales strategy & plan and routes to market, as well as market traction and international expansion.
- The funding roadmap you have devised, your exit strategy, financial projection, and use of funds.
- Your execution plan.
- The team behind it to make it happen, and its credentials and accomplishments.

These criteria are the ones you need to focus on when getting investment ready and preparing the investor pack and pitch. More on this will be found in the following chapters.

Who Is the Right Investor for You?

This is the big yellow school bus that hits you when your tech startup is slowly taking shape. In our experience, we have seen that entrepreneurs tend to go for big investments. But in a short while, they also tend to lose out with investors backing out of the project. So should one go for the aggressive investor? There is no perfect definition of the good investor but there are ways to find the right investor for your tech startup.

We have mentioned already several types of investors in the previous chapter. Let us first take a look at those you can approach for a tech-startup.

- *Angel Investors* (also referred to as business angels) are people with wings in the form of high net worth. They have had past experience in the industry, either at a very senior position or at times as entrepreneurs themselves. They generally have the money to make private investments but with the expectation of very high returns. They are individuals similar to venture capitalists and their direct involvement in your business varies from case to case.

- *Venture Capital Firms or Venture Capitalists (VCs)* provide venture capital, a form of private equity. VCs invest the money that their Limited Partners have committed to a Fund they manage. Many VCs manage several funds, often different ones for early and growth-stage investment. They generally invest in startup companies with high potential for growth. If you are able to convince them that your startup tech company has great potential for growth, you might be able to gain other benefits, too. This includes expert business advice to help pave the path to success for your startup through to exit.

- *Private Equity Firms (PEs)* generally invest in later-stage businesses and buy-outs in turn-around situations.

When you are looking for the investor that is most suited to your business, you would not want investors simply pouring a lot of money into your business, but investors who are truly interested in your tech startup and even guiding you when needed. But that is not as easy as it sounds. Here is what you should be looking for in your potential investor:

- *The Money:* That is what one has to finally get from the investor.
- *The Man:* Experience of the investors in your field.
- *The Preacher:* Even if he is an angel investor, he should actively participate in your business and yet not take complete control of your business.
- *The Mermaid:* The skill of farsightedness with experience and expertise.
- *The Tim Burton:* One who is willing to invest in the craziest of ideas, driven by passion and logic, well reasoned and intuitively sound.

Next, we have to get you ready to convince your potential investor to throw in with you. It is simply an action plan that starts taking shape with each action leading to another:

- *Research:* Get up and get running with all the knowledge you require to convince your investors.
- *Assemble the pitch and perfect it:* Once you have done all the background study for your investor, formulate the pitch. In other words, know what the investor is expecting and requires from you, and show him how well the two of you are suited to bring success to the venture together.

Finally, a good investor would want to see not only your ambition in your business but also the potential in your idea. So you have to get realistic about your financials. Use market research to prove your predictions and your idea's worth.

On the way through the quagmire of obstacles, when it comes to finding the right kind of investor, see that you don't invest in cynicism.

Where Can You Find Angel Investors and VCs?

And the answer is: at home! As discussed in the last chapter, angel investors are the ones who are, well, simply angelic. They come and give you money in the hopes of high returns and will not bother the process of your business directly. On the other hand, venture capitalists are direct and goal-oriented. They not only wish to make money out of your tech startup but also want to play a role in helping with its success.

Regardless of the type of investor you choose, you definitely will need to find them first. The reason why we think you should start from your home first is simple: This is where you can sit back and use your personal computer or laptop. The Internet now has the best platform for finding investors in the form of listing websites. This is where you can get in touch with potential investors first hand.

When you create a profile on a website such as AngelList or Gust, your work in finding angel investors has already begun. There are a few things that you need to keep in mind, however, before creating your profile. Note that there also are websites that have the same kind of platform for venture capitalists. Your profile needs to ignite the interest in angels and venture capitalists in your tech-startup. Therefore, make sure that your profile exudes:

- Honesty

- Farsightedness
- Logical explanation of growth via the business idea
- Knowledge
- Awareness of the technology and the industry you wish to use it in

All in all, investors should be able to perceive that you know what you are talking about. Let's just say that when you are trying to find the right investor, it is important to know the star before you try to reach for it. You should be able to determine how many light years away it is and what kind of space-age technology will take you there. Also, how will you deal with the space debris and neighboring black holes? Most importantly, if you meet a more advanced race of aliens on the way to the same destination, how would you deal with the competition?

Investors today are smarter than they used to be. Hence, communication plays a very important role in getting you the right investor. If the venture capitalists or angel investors are looking for oranges and you ultimately end up communicating the idea of apples, there will be a total disaster, right? Also, building relationships with the potential investors would help you get the right one in no time. It takes a lot of work but ultimately is worth all the trouble.

Also, you could put yourself out there on the Internet and have investors look at your ideas. From social media pages, both professional and general, to blog posts and articles for submission about the industry that your tech startup wishes to cater to, there is a lot you can do to get noticed. The most important thing is to help your potential investors reach you as soon as they are curious about your idea.

The other source is of course your professional and personal network. This seems a much more promising source of finding investors, but remember that when they give you money through the people you know, especially when it comes to angel investors, all the same rules apply. From utter honesty to growth opportunities for the investor, you need to make sure they get all the information.

Crowd Funding
The Next Big Thing?

Crowd funding is perhaps one of the easiest ways to raise funds for your startup. One of the most common practices is to sell a percentage of the ownership of the tech startup on a crowd-funding platform. You won't have to face any major hurdles either; however, funding is legal for people who are recognized investors.

There are different forms of crowd funding:

- *Reward-based crowd funding*, where people give money in return for a reward. As amounts are typically very small, as are rewards, this form may attract a huge number of very small investors to chip in money to make up a sizable but small investment.
- *Equity crowd funding*, where you sell a limited number of shares in your company to equity investors at a given valuation.
- *Debt crowd funding*, where the crowd makes loans to companies seeking funding. It is therefore also referred to as *peer-to-peer lending*.

Equity crowd funding and to a certain extent reward-based crowd funding are probably the forms that best lend themselves to the case of a tech startup in its seed stage. It helps you to raise money through a platform targeted at small investors making the smallest investments and yet adding up to large amount for the fund seeker.

In the case of reward-based crowd funding, investors might not gain direct profit from a share in the business, but they are offered freebies or perhaps the product itself. For instance, if your tech startup wants to sell a specific type of software, the product itself will be expensive to create in the first place. So, you share your idea for the product on the crowd-funding platform. You offer discounts, freebies, or even the finished product, depending on the contribution made via the platform. Say you need $10,000. You might have some people interested in your product willing to offer as much as $400. To those 'investors' you could offer the product as a freebie. In other words, you are pre-selling your product. Then there might be some people who may be interested in a specific freebie you are offering with lower donations, such as a T-shirt with a nice print. So investors get something in return, rather than gaining a say in your business. You are not answerable to them for what your business does from day to day. You also have the option to get some good consumer feedback on your product for free. In addition, you are getting to conduct market research or estimate the success of your product for free.

How to Ensure that People Actually Contribute to Crowd Funding

There are ways in which you can encourage people to invest towards your business. What is key is proper preparation and execution of the crowd-funding campaign. Keep in mind that you need to start preparing your campaign way ahead of its actual launch.

On preparation:

- Make sure your website and Facebook page are up to date, attractive, and reinforce the message of your campaign.
- Prepare the pitch that will be available on the crowd-funding platform.
- Prepare a video pitch, with a basic call to action. It is a must.
- Make sure you have fun freebies being offered.
- Pre-write posts and emails you will later use during the campaign to engage your network.
- Update your contact lists and those of your advocates for use during the campaign.
- Plan the campaign thoroughly (when to release what and where), and don't leave your actions to mere chance, whilst maintaining the flexibility to make adjustments as the campaign evolves.

And on execution:

- See that you have at least a few people contributing initially to get the process started. This is key as it gives a 'social proof' of your tech. Many contributors prefer to follow a lead than taking the lead themselves.
- Constantly engage your network during the campaign, through the (pre-written) posts, emails, newsletters, etc.
- Include the link to your campaign in your emails, newsletters, social profiles, etc.
- Show the progress you make on achieving your funding goal (most platforms do that automatically) to gain the trust of the crowd and create a 'social proof' of your business.
- Make your presence felt online and stay proactive to promote your campaign on free online channels, such as a Facebook or Twitter.

Why is Crowd Funding a Good Idea?

We can list a whole bunch of reasons why crowd funding can benefit your tech startup over other fundraising methods. However, we've decided to go with the most valuable ones:

- You pay the platform a small commission for successful crowd funding, everything else is free.
- You gain the opportunity to evaluate the market for your product prototype.
- You get easier access to capital and, when unable to raise funds, you don't face any losses.
- You can also get ideas for free from investors, in other words access to crowd sourcing.
- You pre-sell to customers who could be potentially loyal customers.
- You get the chance to practice some free PR.

The bottom line is that you are getting a lot of work done on a smaller scale, which would have otherwise taken you a lot of effort. Check out crowd funding, it could be the next big thing for you!

The Funding Roadmap:
How Much Money Should You Ask for?

"How much money should I ask for?" We hear this question all the time. It is obviously one of the most pressing ones for every entrepreneur and a difficult one to get your arms around. We have come across entrepreneurs who ask for as little as $100k and as much as $1m of seed funding. There are Series A funding rounds of as low as $500k, and some that exceed $5m. Some entrepreneurs ask for small amounts on money claiming they have a 'lean startup' and really don't need a lot of money to get going, while those who ask for an amount at the upper end of the spectrum argue that they need will have to front extensive marketing expenses in order to get and maintain traction in the market place. Each one clearly has a point to make. So what is the right amount to ask for?

From an investor's point of view, there is one overarching objective: to maximize the return (see also the chapter on 'What Investors Are Really Looking for'). And there are certain mechanics at work in the capital markets. Angel investors typically invest between $50k and several $100k each, and there are now so-called super angels who invest even larger amounts. Many VCs invest a minimum of $1m, but some now go for smaller rounds as low as $500k or even lower. Imperfections in the market have also created equity gaps, ranges of funding that are hard to raise.

Entrepreneurs need to understand these dynamics for their specific markets and countries. Funding rounds are typically larger in the US, and smaller outside. We often hear entrepreneurs say that they read about company X that has raised (just as an example) $5m in a Series A round of funding despite having only small revenues. That might be true in that specific case, but there are examples for almost any case someone wants to make. What are the lessons someone can learn form such an example? Our answer is simple: none. This is so for a very simple reason: Each case is different, and so is each country.

There is clearly a trade off. As much as raising a large amount is desirable, it is illusive. There is simply not enough funding available and investors in larger rounds want to see tangible market traction before they invest. And founders don't want to give away too much equity in early rounds when their startup's valuation is still low (see also the chapter on 'Valuation: How Much Equity Should You Give Away?').

Asking for too little has also its pitfalls. Entrepreneurs put themselves at risk of running out of runway too early – before achieving important milestones.

That gets them in a really bad position when negotiating the follow-up round. The investment needs to be large enough to allow the company to achieve real value creation and milestones, where progress can be demonstrated with facts and numbers, e.g. growth of client base, revenues, EBITDA, entry in new markets and initial traction, a new release, etc.

Furthermore, fundraising takes time, often months. And the entrepreneur simply cannot afford to be bogged down in too many rounds. His main job is to grow and run the business.

Our recommendation therefore is to plan for a runway of about 12 to 18 months per round. We are of course aware that each case is different, and there are many successful examples of companies with both shorter and longer periods between rounds.

Please also allow us a final word on competition. In the Internet business in particular where the intellectual capital is hard to protect, it is crucial for any company to move fast — very fast. Once your company hits the market and gets traction, competitors will emerge and copy you, and when better funded, they will eventually pass you, and you will lose your first-mover advantage due to insufficient funding. That is the saddest thing that can happen. Make any effort to avoid it!

Valuation:
How Much Equity Should You Give Away?

It seems that valuation is one of the least understood topics despite its importance. We come across entrepreneurs all the time asking this question, and often the valuation they come up with is more a result of guestimating than anything else.

For instance, what's the valuation of an idea? That's a good question, and there is no straightforward answer. Many accelerators who accept pre-seed startups have developed their own rules of thumb and have defined a range for the equity stake they take in return for a fixed amount of cash and a service package they offer.

For a seed or early-stage company, valuation becomes more complex. Some entrepreneurs use discounted cash flow (DCF) to calculate the net present value (NPV) of their company. Whilst this is a widely-used approach in business, it lends itself more to mature businesses that have a set of historical data the valuation can be based on: market size, market share, growth rates, margins, etc. But what reliable data set is available for a business or market that is in its inception? How can we know for a market that is currently emerging what the customer uptake will be, how many competitors will enter, and at which price point it will arrive when maturing? As a fact, few investors rely on DCF.

Other entrepreneurs use more accounting-driven methods and try to assign a monetary value to the time and effort spent when building a first product release. Somehow, they also assign a valuation to the intellectual property they have created. Both methods, however, are not suitable because of their backward-looking character.

Other entrepreneurs look at comparable companies and try to find similar cases to their own, cases that have recently received funding at a certain valuation. That might lead to certain estimates, but again there is all reason to be cautious since the details of the transaction and the company's figures are typically not known to the public.

Still others simply guestimate the value of their company based on intangibles like the experience of their team and differentiation of their proposition.

So if none of these methods leads to satisfactory results, what is the right approach? To answer this question, you need to consider the investor's return expectations. As pointed out in the chapter 'What Investors Are Really Looking for', investors look for certain return multiples of their investment at the point of exit, with the multiple depending on the stage of the investment, among other considerations.

Therefore, investors will simulate potential exit values, based on a series of factors: comparable exits, typical revenue and EBITDA-multiples in that specific industry, valuation of companies that have recently received funding and are now at a later stage, and some others. Then they calculate the potential dilution they will face during the lifetime of their investment (thus the importance of the funding roadmap, see the last chapter). By doing so, they will arrive at a percentage of equity they will need to take in order to achieve their desired return multiple, and based on the funding the entrepreneur asks for, they can calculate the valuation pre- and post-money.

What does that mean for the entrepreneur? Above all, it is about preparing a credible business case. This is fundamentally about the revenue and EBITDA projections for the years to come. The emphasis needs to be on being credible. Although business case modeling is a somewhat theoretical exercise, there needs to be absolute clarity of the underlying assumptions, which have to be expressed in terms that make sense in real life, e.g. number of users, customers, countries the company is present in, clicks, units sold, sales channels activated, etc.

Still, nobody has a crystal ball. With startups being a high-risk business, investors will run different scenarios and make adjustments for themselves to your numbers. You should do the same.

Becoming Investment Ready

What's the big deal? Becoming investment ready is essentially writing a business plan and investor pitch (see also respective chapters on 'Business Plan 101' and 'The Pitch'). The business plan is basically a business case enhanced by all kinds of considerations on product development, marketing, sales, and execution. On pitching in particular there is plenty of training material and advice available at the entrepreneur's fingertips. Still, we have seen huge differences between really compelling plans and pitches and mediocre ones. With funding in short supply, every entrepreneur needs to aim for the best to stand out from the pack.

Unfortunately, there is no guarantee for success. But there are many ways to fail, some of which we have come across, for instance:

- Business plans that are more than 60 pages long, that would require an average person to spend several hours to read and understand.
- Business plans that show no relationship between the actions the plan defines and the business case numbers it is supposed to produce.
- Plans that lack specifics on customer acquisition cost, marketing expenses, conversation rates, etc.
- Growth projections based on wishful thinking rather than specific market penetration and expansion plans.
- Lack of ambition to grow the business beyond the entrepreneur's comfort zone.
- Unbalanced teams with clear lack of crucial skills.
- Pitches long on number of slides, but short on content.
- Unrealistic funding requests (see chapter on 'The Funding Roadmap: How Much Money Should You Ask for?').

It is key for the entrepreneur to put himself into the shoes of an investor and understand what he is looking for:

- An easy-to-understand outline of the product and the real problem it solves or desire it satisfies.
- A clear, competitive differentiation against current competitors and barriers to entry for future ones.
- A compelling marketing and sales strategy and plan to show how to get traction and at what cost.
- An ambitious international expansion plan to become a true international player with a strong presence in the market where the exit is going to happen.
- A credible business case that reflects the assumptions behind the business and its growth and demonstrates a clear path to exit.
- A well-balanced team with all required skill sets and a proven track record

of accomplishments, to give confidence to an investor that the team will get stuff done.

- Writing the document is the easy part, thinking it through is not. Preparing it takes weeks or months of collaboration among the team, picking the brains of advisors, mentors, and friends, and tapping into their own experience.

Business planning is not a theoretical exercise either. Market testing the assumptions as soon as possible is key, to allow pivoting early on.

We recommend to go step-by-step through the points we made above on investors' expectations and come up with compelling and concrete answers to the many questions that investors will have. In the next two chapters, you will find a list of investor questions that need to be addressed in your pack and pitch.

The planning typically passes through a series of iterations and will eventually be documented in an investor pack and a pitch document. These are probably the most important documents in the life of a startup. As the saying goes: "You have only one chance to make a bad impression." You have one shot with each investor to make a good impression and get his attention and interest to learn more about your startup. Please keep this in mind when preparing.

The Investor Pack

Part of becoming investment ready consists of thinking through the strategy the business is taking and translating it into a business plan which you use when you raise funding (see also the previous chapter on 'Becoming Investment Ready'). This plan needs to be presented in form of an investor pack to potential investors.

There is no standard format, and we have seen a wide range of documents entrepreneurs typically prepare. Many develop a text-based document that is rather verbose and often more than 50 pages long. Some entrepreneurs produce videos and extensive product pitches. Some write executive summaries, others don't.

All entrepreneurs use spreadsheets to calculate their numbers, but again we find a wide range of formats are being used. Some entrepreneurs forecast numbers for two years into the future while others apply a longer forecast period. Some entrepreneurs provide a very granular level of detail, whilst others refrain to calculating high-level figures.

Entrepreneurs also produce a pitch presentation. Again, styles are quite diverse. Some entrepreneurs choose more graphical layouts, while others prefer more bullet-style texts or other more text-heavy formats. The length of pitches also varies formidably.

So what makes a good investor pack? To come up with the answer, you first and foremost must understand your target audience – the investor – and what he is interested in (see also the chapter on 'What Investors Are Really Looking for'). The documentation needs to focus on those aspects, and you must be aware that they might be quite different from those a potential client, partner, or the general audience want to know.

Secondly, you need to understand how investors operate. A qualified investor looks at as many opportunities as he possibly can and uses filters that allow him to dig deeper only into those opportunities he views as high potential and in line with his expectations. It is therefore important to make it as easy as possible for an investor to understand and assess the opportunity in order to get his attention and interest to engage in a conversation with you.

For that reason, it is imperative to follow the 5Cs of an investor pack:

- **Clear**
- **Complete**
- **Concise**
- **Compelling**
- **Credible**

We highly recommend you produce an executive summary that can be read and understood in three minutes and entice the investor to look into the details of your pitch and plan. The content needs to answer his most pressing questions. Here is an open list:

- What real-life problem does your product address, or which desire does it satisfy?
- How is it resolved or satisfied today?
- How does your product resolve or satisfy it?
- How is your product different from your competitors'?
- What barriers of entry are you going to create to limit future competition?
- How do you create awareness of your product in the market place?
- How do you sell it?
- Who do you sell it to?
- What routes to market do you use?
- What revenue streams do you have?
- What are the price points you are able or expect to be able to charge?
- What is the expected or real customer acquisition cost and customer lifetime value?
- How will you grow your business abroad?
- How do your plans translate into your financial projections?
- What is your exit strategy?
- What is your funding roadmap and how does it align with the technology

roadmap and growth roadmap?
- How are you going to use the funds raised?
- What return do you expect to achieve for your investors?
- Who is on your team and advisory board?
- What are the team members' skills and accomplishments?
- What milestones have you reached so far?
- What are the immediate plans after funding?

With respect to the style, it should be fresh, attractive, and above all, authentic. It is about getting someone invested in you and your company, and the more authentic you are the better you get your message across.

The Pitch

You can't simply go to the investor, show your innovative idea, and expect the investor to fund your startup. The investor would not only want to find innovation in the product, but would like to know whether that innovation would be really useful to the people and help everyone make a profit. It is like having a superhero on the streets whose superpower is laying eggs at will. Since we have taken the idea of a superhero, let's just say that your tech startup is the superhero and you need to convince the people of your city that this superhero is worth their time and money. For this scenario, the city folk are the investors.

How to Sell Your Superhero (Tech Startup Idea) to the City People (Investors)?

Superheroes, AKA tech startup ideas, might be very strong when in action but highly vulnerable to criticism. The city people, AKA the investors, would not want to waste their time or money on something that will not give them any output. So they will naturally be very critical. If the superhero makes even the tiniest wrong move, he will be criticized for it for life. So it is a good idea to be very careful to present the superhero to the city folks cautiously.

- ***Don't just boast about the superpowers and their potential, show them***: When you are selling the superhero, you have to show the superpowers and their potential to the city folk. This means that your investors will not be interested in simple facts and figures about the tech startup or how innovative it is. You will have to pitch in action. This involves a lot of homework, which essentially means market research. Knowing the supervillains, AKA the competition in the market, is an important part of your pitch. Finding the strength in your idea is what the investors will be looking for.
- ***Speak through actions and let the superhero do the talking***: Keep the pitch short and simple. However, make sure that the pitch is impactful. You

need to be able to quickly create a favorable impression on the potential investors. A superhero never talks too much in public, instead he relies on simple but highly impressionable dialogue, such as "I am Batman." It not only answers the question but also creates a powerful impact on the city folks.

- **A reality check**: No superheroes are immortal – they can be put down. So make sure that you are very clear about your tech startup's potential. Do not show them a big figure that is not only unachievable but may make your investors lose faith in your business idea. Instead, show what you are capable of. This is one of the reasons why superheroes first turn up as vigilantes, rather than simply declaring their superhero presence before they have done something. If you do not have past experience, then show a demo. A small demo of your tech startup and consumer feedback can do the trick for your pitch.
- **Heroism takes time to happen**: It takes time to make any business idea work, let alone the tech startup world. So explain to your investors how you wish to revolutionize the market with your product, step by step. Remember how every superhero movie shows us what the superhero is capable of, one action at a time.

Entrepreneurs, who have initially started with nothing and yet made it big, have showcased their superpowers to the world in the right way and that is what you have to do for your pitch.

The bottom line is: Invest in your investor...and invest in your pitch!

Business Plan 101

A lot of business ideas start with a light bulb and end in a business plan on a piece of paper. Even if the business plan starts on a piece of toilet paper, it is yours and it can and needs to be developed into a proper business plan. It is not about having the perfect business plan but evaluating and researching your way to one. Planning simply ensures that you think thoroughly about factors that could impact your tech startup, research facts that you are unsure of, and finally look at your idea critically and modify the idea accordingly. Business planning takes time. The more time you invest in developing a strong foundation for your business, the lower your chances will be of you ending up with an expensive disaster.

The Basic Format of a Business Plan

When you are writing out a business plan, you need to first organize your thinking. It is best to have a blueprint of what you need to put down in black and white. There is a basic template that can be followed to write a business plan. You can always keep adding to and modifying the plan as your insights and needs change.

- **Executive summary**: Although this will be the introduction to your plan, write it right at the end. It should include the gist of all the fundamentals of the proposed business plan.
- **General tech business description**: This includes the mission statement for your tech startup, the goals that it intends to achieve, the philosophy of the business, industry description, competencies and strengths of the founder(s), and of course the legal ownership form.
- **Products and services being offered**: This where you explain the products or services that you intend to offer. You will need to explain what problems they solve or desires they satisfy, as well as mention the technical specifications, product features and benefits; provide graphical representations of the product(s), sales brochures, and other appendices. Under this heading, also mention the elements that would give you a competitive edge as well as threats to the ideas.
- **Marketing plan**: This encompasses a very broad spectrum and you will need to include various types of information. Start with your market research and its conclusions. Also, mention how the market research has helped you understand the potential of the overall market. The elements that need to be described here include:
  - The economics of the industry
  - The market and target audience
  - The **4Ps** of marketing: Product, Price, Place, and Promotion and their relation with each other
  - Your promotional budget, marketing strategy, and channels of distribution
  - The sales forecast.
- **Operational plan**: This includes more structured issues, such as production, the personnel handling production, legal environment, location, credit policies, supplies, and inventory. Management of the account structure has to be mentioned here as well.
- **Management and organization**: You will need to provide a description of the professionals and advisory support for the business, such as the board of directors, management advisory board, accountants, bankers, attorneys, consultants, mentors, and even insurance agents.
- **Personal financial statement**: This will consist all the details of the various shareholders and their financial details.
- **Startup expenses and capitalization**: This includes expense estimation not only for the tech startup build, but also the eventual expenses you expect to incur in its day-to-day operations.
- **Financial plan**: Projection of profit and loss, the opening day balance sheet and financial details such as break-even analysis should be mentioned here.
- **Appendices**: This will include the information sources for all that has helped you create the business plan.

Refining the plan will be the final chapter and will consist of the overall economic outlook, management of the whole production process and, most importantly, the handling of legal issues.

About Metrics

When you have the right kind of metrics aligned to your business, you can actually reach your targets more efficiently. For example, in August 2013 a Norwegian duo of brothers called Ylvis came up with a viral video on YouTube. The song was hilarious and reached online audiences for the ridiculous lyrics in the song. The song is called *What Does the Fox Say*? This video, a promotional tactic for their talk show in Norway, witnessed 15 million views!

The video did exactly what it was meant to do: make people watch the talk show. But millions of viewers, who would probably not have gotten to see the show even if they wanted to, are now getting to see it. So should we count the number of views of the video or the target rating point of the show after the video was released? Or should we count the number of times the IP addresses from which the video was accessed were based in Norway?

Metrics are all about making the basic judgments that help you measure the eventual success or failure of your tech startups. You need to be able to track each division or department in your company, along with individual progress against very detailed, measurable goals. This is the best way to ensure that management is effective when it comes to the fundamentals of the business.

How to Choose the Right Metrics?

The way to make an informed decision is to first find answers to some basic questions, such as:

- What are the most important things that will impact the business in the first year of its establishment?
- What are the detailed revenue objectives, annually as well as quarterly, in the same year?
- What criteria should you use to measure success in the first year of the startup's establishment?

Common Mistakes in Choosing Metrics & How to Avoid Them

To make sure that you don't fall prey to the mistakes often made by entrepreneurs while choosing metrics, here are some points to keep in mind while making your choice:

- Don't choose metrics with incorrect or incomplete data.
- Avoid metrics that are complex or difficult to understand and describe.
- There will be some metrics that complicate the operational process and are tedious. Avoid such metrics.
- Metrics should not cause employees to act against the interest of the company.

What to Do After Choosing the Metrics?

You can use various SaaS (Software-as-a-Service) applications to pull out information and perform data analysis that enables you to measure your progress on each business goal. There are a lot of options you will find online for this purpose.

This next step is very important. You need to share the metrics with all the employees in your company. Unless they are aware of their goals, how will they work to achieve them? Each individual employee should be aware of his role in making your tech startup successful. Also, ask for feedback from your employees.

Leaders should lead by example. This means that accountability also includes the entrepreneur himself. So share your own goals with the team and demonstrate your sincerity to maintaining transparency. This will help build trust in you as a leader as well as faith in your business idea.

Business priorities change with time and so should the metrics. Therefore, keep revaluating your metrics for better results. In other words, review, monitor, and refine metrics to ensure that you are basing business decisions on the right analysis.

Remember, metrics may change regularly and may bring challenges with them, but they also help you keep up with your competition and the rest of the industry.

FOUR

On Team
and Execution

I Have a Lean Startup

Congratulations! The lean startup concept has become very popular since Eric Ries published his ground breaking book The Lean Startup in 2012. There are events and training sessions on the lean startup held around the globe, and new books are being published, among them The Lean Entrepreneur by Brant Cooper and Patrick Vlaskovits, published in 2013. So when you consider your startup being lean, you are right with the trend.

But what does it really mean to be a lean startup? Some entrepreneurs believe it is fundamentally about spending as little as possible. It sounds like a good idea; investors and entrepreneurs will get a higher return when the company spends less and achieves the same. But do these startups really achieve the same?

We have come across entrepreneurs who were proud of having managed to attract hundreds or thousands of visits to their sites despite spending virtually zero on marketing. What they don't see and say, however, is how many more visits they would have received when they had spent more on marketing, and how much faster would they have grown their revenues as a consequence. And growing revenues (and profits!) as fast as possible is the name of the game.

Don't forget, the investor and the entrepreneur receive their return at the exit event, and although there is no simple formula to calculate the company's valuation at the point of exit, there is a clear correlation between valuation and revenues and profits. So the objective should not be to spend as little as possible, but to grow as fast as possible while optimizing the use of funds to do so.

But how do you find the right balance? First, the more you spend on revenue-generating activities, the better. In other words, you need to spend as little as possible on overhead.

Secondly, you need to come to grips with the effectiveness of the capital deployed, and you do that through the use of metrics (see more on metrics in a previous chapter). You need to understand:

- For each additional dollar you spend on marketing, how much additional revenue and EBITDA will it generate?
- What is your customer acquisition cost and customer lifetime value (see separate chapters)?
- What is your right marketing mix to maximize the bang you get for your buck?

In other words, you need to maximize the impact of each dollar spent. This is easier said than done and you will need to go through various iterations and trial-and-error cycles. This leads us to yet another concept of the lean startup: the ability to pivot. So instead of pouring resources into an activity which you are not sure will really help grow the business, test that activity's outcome early on and make the necessary adjustments, and do this pretty quickly.

Please also be aware of your competitors. They also need to grow their businesses and often intend to do so by eating market share from you. Imagine you have an Internet startup and your closest competitor, although trailing behind you on revenues and number of customers, starts spending significantly more on marketing than you do and does it in a smart and effective way. As a consequence, his revenues will grow faster than yours, and the day will come when he surpasses you. And you will lose your first-mover advantage, should you have had it before. You don't really what this to happen, do you?

Consequently, you need to design your funding roadmap accordingly (see a separate chapter to get more insight on the funding roadmap). Some entrepreneurs try to raise only small amounts of money, enough to survive and grow modestly. But they forget that growing fast is the name of the game and that often requires more than modest funding.

About the Founders.
Who Should Be the CEO?

Who shall be the chief executive officer (CEO)? This is a seemingly simple question with a straightforward answer: one of the founders, obviously; the one who had the initial idea. But is the answer really that easy?

Let us first understand what the role of the CEO entails. Naturally, the CEO has the overall responsibility for all business concerns and in relationship with all stakeholders. He is accountable for delivering value to the shareholders and meeting all obligations of the company. Wikipedia defines the role of the CEO or Managing Director (MD) as: "Typically, the CEO/MD has responsibilities as a director, decision maker, leader, manager, and executor. The communicator role can involve the press and the rest of the outside world, as well as the organization's management and employees; the decision-making role involves high-level decisions about policy and strategy. As a leader of the company, the CEO/MD advises the board of directors, motivates employees, and drives change within the organization. As a manager, the CEO/MD presides over the organization's day-to-day operations."

In our view, the major task of the CEO in a technology startup is to keep the boat afloat, or in other words: make sure the company does not run out of runway. As we know, technology startups are high-risk businesses, and as such suffer a high mortality rate. Clearly, the CEO together with his leadership team needs to do all he possibly can to avoid his company running out of cash and goes bust, or as some investors call it, have an 'involuntary exit'.

Investors are fully aware of that situation. Therefore, there is a common belief that they invest in the team rather than the product. There is certainly some truth in this thinking, but the reality is they invest in the business. And a business needs more than just a great team; it needs a product that addresses a real market need or satisfies a real desire and is positioned in a way that it wins against its competitors. A business also needs to have a plan to take the idea to market and the capabilities to commercialize it. A business needs to be sufficiently funded to be able to execute its plan and be able to attract investors by offering them a compelling investment opportunity and attractive returns. Nothing is sadder than a high-potential but chronically underfunded business. And finally, a business needs to make all this happen. And it is the role of the CEO to orchestrate all activities to make all this happen.

This sounds very difficult, and in fact it is. Therefore, what we are looking for in a CEO is a series of character traits:

- Business savvy
- Ability to listen
- Bias for action
- Authenticity

Let's discuss each of these, one at a time.

Having business savvy is a prerequisite that comes without saying for anyone who builds and runs a business. More often than not, however, tech startups are being founded by people with a technology background and founders often lack business skills in marketing, sales, finance, or leadership. That's not their fault, but it is what it is. In such a case, the founders have only two options: either they acquire these skills themselves, and do that fairly quickly, or alternatively find a co-founder or hire a CEO who has these skills to run the business for them.

The ability to listen is another character trait that is absolutely essential. Why? The reason is simple. The task of the CEO in a tech startup is enormous: running the ship in unchartered territory on a shoestring budget without running out of runway. That's what successful entrepreneurs do and many have done. But some CEOs also tend to have inflated egos, believing they know it all. And many articles and events foster this belief, making entrepreneurs believe that they are the ones to change the world. But nobody is perfect and the fact of the matter is that there are many people out there who know certain aspects of the business better than the entrepreneur himself, people who have a specific experience in a certain field or have done it before. Many of them are willing to give honest advice and often are flattered by being asked. All it needs is an entrepreneur willing and able to listen.

Bias for action is another essential character trait. This seems to be an obvious one. Unfortunately, we have come across many entrepreneurs who talk when they have to act, stall when they have to move, and doubt when they have to leap forward. In a tech startup you need to be moving – always. And that's why investors look for entrepreneurs with a proven track record of achievements as a proxy for the entrepreneur's ability to get stuff done.

And finally, we believe that **authenticity** is key. Entrepreneurs are constantly selling: selling their business case to investors, selling their products to clients, selling their vision to the media, and selling job opportunities, that require hard work for little pay, to future employees. We, the general public, hear polished party line talk and get flooded with gobbledygook all the time. We don't want to get more, from anyone, let alone the entrepreneur. What we want is what sets a great entrepreneur apart: being authentic.

Technical and Business Skills

What skill sets does a tech startup need? This seems to be one of those questions with an obvious answer: both technical and business skills, of course.

Why is it then that so many tech startups lack one or the other?

As a matter of fact, many startups start with an entrepreneur with a background in technology and an idea for a product. Such entrepreneurs are generally very good at what they are doing; they like what they are doing and they have learned, studied, and practiced what they like: developing technologies.

Of course, nobody is perfect and we often find a lack of business skills in tech startups; skills such as marketing, sales, finance, recruiting, leadership, etc.

As we have seen, startup success is about building successful businesses, not just developing great products or technologies. The saddest thing about these technologies is that many of them never see the light of day and eventually get buried in a laboratory or garage because nobody managed to create a successful business for them.

Investors know that and therefore look for a balanced skill set in the startups they invest in. But how can gaps in business skills be compensated? There are plenty of possibilities.

Startups can seek business mentors and advisors. Many universities, startup schools, and incubators run mentoring programmes. Accelerators are often mentoring-based. Investors also like to see startups constitute an advisory board with members who are experts in the respective industry and can bring real experiences to the table, real experiences from which the entrepreneur can learn.

Startups can also get co-funders on board with the complementary skills that are lacking. Or they can hire professionals with strong capabilities to fill the gap, but (very important!) need to compensate them generously in order to retain and minimize the risk of losing them.

There are also cases, although less frequent, of entrepreneurs who wish to start a technology business without having a technology background. Many business schools run entrepreneurship programmes or venture labs and encourage their students to embark on an entrepreneurial career path. This can be an attractive alternative for many students in an economy where large companies cannot provide job security any longer and individuals prefer to take their fate into their own hands. Often business school students lack technology skills and unfortunately business schools in many cases are not connected with technical universities. What can these entrepreneurs do?

In the best case, there is some kind of matchmaking programme to help trying to find the right skill combination and matching people with complementary skills and compatible interests in order to 'manufacture serendipity'. However, these programmes do not always exist.

An option is to outsource technology development to an outside firm (see the chapter specifically dedicated to discussing the pros and cons of outsourcing). In this case, however, the entrepreneur is running the risk of not 'owning' the technical know-how and potentially 'losing' it for not having it fully locked in inside the company.

There are also technology incubators that have been launched specifically to complement the team of a startup with technical resources and skills in return for an equity stake in the company. That model might be attractive due to alignment of goals and commitments, with the incubator effectively becoming a co-founder who will stay with the business until the exit, sharing the success and risk alike.

And finally, in an ideal situation the entrepreneur may find a co-founder with the technical background so desperately needed. But of course, this is more a question of luck than anything else.

Who Should Be CFO?

If avoiding running out of runway is the most formidable task of the CEO, managing the numbers behind the business to assist the CEO in this task is the job of the chief financial officer (CFO). What does that job entail?

According to Wikipedia, the CFO is "a corporate officer primarily responsible for managing the financial risks of the corporation. This officer is also responsible for financial planning and record keeping, as well as financial reporting to higher management. In some sectors the CFO is also responsible for analysis of data. The title is equivalent to finance director."

The CFO's responsibilities therefore include to:

- Prepare and update the financial statements, to give the CEO in each and every moment a clear view of the situation in terms of financial resources and obligations, to enable him - on the basis of facts - to assess and manage the risk of running out of runway, as well as to meet record keeping and reporting requirements to shareholders and governmental organizations.
- Provide expert advice on any finance-related issue of the company.
- Act as the interface with the company accountant and oversee the activities required to meet all record keeping, reporting, and everything tax-related as well as other legal obligations related to finance.
- Prepare the financial case for any fundraising activity.

This sounds like a big job, and it is. So what is the best way to fill the CFO role in a tech startup that is short of cash in its early years?

Let us first understand what investors are looking for. As we pointed out in other chapters, investors look for three things: the exit, the exit, and the exit – the liquidity event that generates the return for their Limited Partners and themselves. Therefore, any business case needs to address this overarching goal in a compelling and credible way. Investors are also interested in understanding the underlying assumptions of any business case, as well as the metrics to see how the business is performing in the real world rather than going through a theoretical exercise.

So producing the business case is at the heart of the CFO's role? The answer is definitely yes. But we have also come across entrepreneurs who delegate this activity entirely to the CFO. This is a big mistake.

It is the CEO who needs to take ownership of the business case, it is he who has to pitch and defend it in front of investors. It is he who needs to know his numbers inside out. Remember, it is he who needs to keep the boat afloat and do everything to avoid the company running out of runway. And it is he who is accountable for delivering the return to the shareholders. The CFO, however, needs to assist the CEO in managing and controlling the numbers.

To hire the right CFO, you have several options depending in the stage of the company:

At a very early stage, the CEO, assuming that he has sufficient background in finance, can act as CFO, and work with an accountancy firm for record keeping, reporting, and in many cases, payroll.

When the company grows, it might be advisable to hire a part-time CFO, with a dedication of maybe one or two days a week. There are excellent professionals available in the marketplace who offer these type of arrangements.

At a later stage, when the workload justifies it, you will eventually hire a full-time CFO.

How to Attract the Best People and Grow the Team

If the best people could be attracted with money, then all business schools specializing in Human Resources and the role of a Human Resources department would cease to exist! It definitely attracts some people but not everyone you are looking for in your team. So here are some ways to ensure that you attract the right people to build a team with an invincible spirit.

Attracting the Best People to Grow Your Team

There is so much to the team building process than simply looking through résumés, and yet we find it difficult to believe that recruiting the right person is difficult. It is a task that can literally make or break your company. The teams you put together will be pillars on which you build your tech startup. So here is how to find and attract those pillars:

- You will need the same approach for attracting the best people as you will have for finding and convincing anyone to raise funds for your startup. They have to believe that your business idea will work. Statistics will not convince them as much as the utility of your product might. Explain the growth potential to your team members once they become part of your business. Do not be afraid of people raising too many questions about your idea. Sometimes, your confidence in addressing these questions and not simply answering them can win you great people. Also, sometimes the potential team member asking too many annoying questions can be your most enthusiastic recruit. Why? Simply because he is interested in your idea enough to think over it on many levels.

- Add benefits beyond money and perks. Let's just go beyond the Home Rental Allowances and medical insurance coverage. Let's think of out-of-the-box ideas. Google offers their employees a 'Nap-pod', where employees can take 40 winks without having to get too tired and provide only average quality work. So they have a stylish chair with a top that can cover your head while you take a nap on the office premises. Not only does it show that you care about your team's well being but also that you really care about the quality of work. But then again you aren't Google... yet! So instead, get a corporate membership for a gym close to your office and offer employees a free gym facility.

- Look for smart workers over hard workers. Hard working is good but it might fail to provide the results and end up as an absolute waste of energy. Instead of looking for people who will be able to work long hours, it is best to look at the most productive hours of their day.

Finally, it is after all a little bit about the money, if not all about the money. Find out what the current salary rates are in the market and decide your budget accordingly. Also, note that if you offer salaries below the going rate, chances are that you may not end up with the best talent, or worse you might end up with the best people who lose their initiative at work because the lower rate acts as a mental barrier for the team member to give 100%.

One last word; while qualifications are something to look for, attitude is something you cannot ignore. Skills can be learned on the job. But unless one comes in with the right attitude, all the qualifications in the world won't help make that team member an asset to your business.

How to Get Non-Executives and Advisors on Board

While your executives are getting things up and rolling for your organization, you cannot miss out on the people who see the bigger picture and contribute to it through three very important factors: development of strategy and planning, development of organization and community, and development of fundraising and support. Now, that is a lot of work to be done, but when you need multiple minds to get involved, non-executives and advisors can be made much use of.

Why is it Important to Choose Non-Execs Wisely?

"More often than not, a CEO is merely a puppet whose strings are pulled by a board of directors." - Mokokoma Mokhonoana.

This is another risk when it comes to getting non-execs and advisors. However, this risk can be avoided. Mr. Mokhonoana, a social criticism and philosophical author from South Africa, does mention, "more often than not." Hence, you could be an entrepreneur who works together with the non-execs while not being stomped all over by the board. The first step for this is to choose the right kind of people.

How Do You Choose Non-Execs and Advisors?

Perhaps buying a horse is easier than choosing the right kind of non-executives for your tech startup. But there are factors, which if kept in mind can help ensure that you do not choose the wrong ones or what we like to call the "The Court Jesters": those who will show you all the problems and criticize the ideas but never speak a word about what the solution can be. You definitely don't want that, although those people can be highly entertaining.

Here are some tips:

- *The purpose of having non-execs in your company*: Do not have non-execs on board because we asked you to have some. You would need to know their purpose and the requirement for the company first. Do you have them for the developmental purposes that we mentioned in an earlier chapter? Or do they add business skills and experience?

- *The purpose of having advisors*: Consider the areas in which you need advice for your startup. Once you know this, you need to choose advisors who specialize in those areas. At the same time, each board member should be compatible to work with the others. Once they have entered in a conference or are serving their purpose, all you would need to worry about is the task at hand.

- *Make your expectations clear:* Whether you have them for money or you have them for support in strategy and planning or even for legal issues, make what you are expecting from them very clear. The transparency in expectations helps you encourage them to keep to their commitments easily…even if their role is mere entertainment.

- *Ensure confidentiality*: If there are things about the company that you do not wish to reveal to the public, then ask them to them sign a Non-Disclosure Agreement. This could be necessary for confidentiality in trade secrets and confidential information that run the risk of being leaking out.

- **Get standard Non-Executive-Director contracts signed:** If your advisors also play the role of Directors in your business, you must have your corporate lawyer or legal advisor draw up a Non-Executive-Director contract that gets signed and stamped. Non-execs should be open to signing one.

A lot of people think that non-execs are useless people who sit around a table and say why your idea will not work. Sure, you want that, but ultimately you would also want a person who supports you in seeking and executing solutions.

Once your advisors are on board, don't forget to conduct their induction and appraisals at regular intervals.

Pay Your Staff, Give Them Equity, or Both?

Incentives play a crucial role in keeping the staff motivated at all times and your tech startup is no exception. Financially, both cash and equity will add to the cost to the company in the same way. It can be also broken down into ratios, if you wish to award employees with incentives both ways at the same time. However, the outcomes will be varied. To understand this situation better, let's look at the benefits in all three cases.

Why Pay Your Staff?

When people are joining an organization and being paid a salary, they are in fact looking for stability when it comes to finances. The ultimate goal for any employee will be earning his or her living. Hence, if they are rewarded for working more or performing better than minimally required, it will not only increase the ROI of your staff in a tech-startup but will also motivate them to work better.

For several people, receiving an incentive over their salary also adds to their sense of prestige when being associated with your company. It helps them understand their importance and play their role. In a small company, where the brand name is not yet known and the stakes are high, one of the best ways to attract good people is the pay. However, your budget may be tight at the beginning, so payment through incentives can actually help save on paying big salaries and yet attract good people. Sometimes, incentives are not necessarily paid through cash alone. Vouchers, competitive incentives, and target-achievement rewards may also come in handy.

Why Give Your Staff Equity?

When you give incentives through equity to employees rather than cash, you drive more ownership for their role in the company. How? Because the financial interests of your employees become more dependent on the business, which will eventually drive better performance.

Also, the accountability of a shareholder is typically higher. And employees are also playing a broader and more varied role in a tech startup than in a big, established company where the work of each employee is confined to each person's area of specialization.

In present times, income over one's base salary has become a necessity for many to maintain a good standard of living. Therefore, employees would expect incentives through equity for their performance. This helps attract a larger pool of talent, without leading to huge cash outlays for the company.

Why Do Both?

Well, when you opt for both you simply get the best of both worlds and what the one lacks is compensated with the combined strength of both. One could compare it to a scenario where you take extra ownership where you are not only held accountable for the company's profits and losses, but also getting a reward for the upside, i.e. enhancing the company's value since you too are a partial owner. When you have helped create something, you want it to shine and when one has further benefits from better performance of his company, he would surely have more reasons to put the company's interests before his own. In other words,

"Money is a good servant but a bad master." - Francis Bacon, Sr.

So when you are allowing your employees to be the master of the money they make, they will be not be driven by money but the fact that:

"Money won't create success, the freedom to make it will." - Nelson Mandela

Team Building 101

"None of us is as smart as all of us" - Kenneth H. Blanchard

One would think of it as a meeting of minds over a set of targets, but teams are much more than targets and outcomes. They are a mix of art and science, when it comes to building a team that is cohesive and cooperative, even when the going gets tough. People often confuse the concept of team building with how to work with a team. Teambuilding is best done in steps that can be followed by every team leader and understood by every other team member.

Steps to Building Great Teams

I believe that a team that gets along with one another is a rare, yet wonderful thing. But this is simply not sufficient. It is better to have a team that gets along well enough to, if necessary, constructively criticize one another to achieve the goals of the organization. The goals of a team come before any individual members. Once each member recognizes and practices this in his work, the team is believed to have enough rapport to achieve the most difficult, long-term goals together.

Here is a simple 7-step approach to building great teams.

Step 1:

Have the team take ownership: Your team or teams should consist of people who take responsibility for their individual roles as well as hold themselves accountable for their performance as part of a whole. In other words, the strongest link in the team should be as accountable for the performance of the team as the weakest link is.

Step 2:

Recognize individual strengths: It is always best to choose team members with specific individual skills and knowledge. It is also not a bad idea to have people with different perspectives and ideologies. In fact, it gives you insight into the team's work from different angles that like-minded people may not have thought of.

Step 3:

Unify the team with a mission: It is very important to establish a unified purpose for the team, regardless of individual roles in the team. Once you have chosen a diversified team, it is above all your other duties to make the team members aware of this purpose or mission that they will achieve together. This will further help you motivate the team and enhance its performance, since the team members will understand that, regardless of his individual role in the team, each member is accountable for his performance as part of the whole team.

Step 4:

Explain each role in the game play: Organize every team member's role in a way that their importance and role is directly evident in the team's performance. Members therefore cease to become individuals and work as a team.

Step 5:

Put commitments forward to each other: Each member needs to make individual commitments to achieve his goals. In the case of a tech startup, it could be a whole department that can be taken as a team. The sub-teams, AKA members, have to commit to each other and let each other know that they will get work done accordingly and meet their commitments.

Step 6:

Choose team leaders: You have to find a person who is as committed to the team's goals as you are as the entrepreneur. The leadership qualities that make you a great team leader would be applicable. Yes, the one who leads from the front and leads from the back, as discussed in a later chapter.

Step 7:

Address grievances individually: As a team leader, you have to understand that individual issues to keep up to the commitments need to be kept private and therefore, all addressed by yourself individually. If a team member fails to commit to work enough to achieve the team's goals, then seek more commitment from a member who can achieve those commitments.
Here is something we have learned over time: Get rid of people who play the blame game, but work on the people who say and practice "My bad, I'll rectify it." Sometimes, it is a tough thing to do, but a person who is accountable for his actions, good or bad, will always be a great team member.

Boiling the Ocean

The life of an entrepreneur can be very rewarding, but more often than not he is asked to do the impossible: Deliver exponential growth to achieve a high exit value in a short period of time and do so on a shoestring budget.

It comes to no surprise that entrepreneurs run the risk of losing focus. The founders cannot afford to hire many employees, so everyone in the company has to perform multiple functions. And deadlines are tight. On top of all that, the idea of going after as broad a market as possible is genuinely tempting… to achieve the desired growth rapidly. Often, this is nothing more than wishful thinking.

We have seen entrepreneurs who launch their product too early in order to win clients as soon as possible, when the product is actually not market-ready. Although we definitely are strong advocates of lean startup methods and highly recommend any startup to get real market feedback as soon as possible through early field trials with real-life users, commercially launching a product too early in the worst case will lead to instant rejection even by the early adopters – a fatal outcome.

We have also come across entrepreneurs who do exactly the opposite. In striving to create the perfect solution, they keep it in a sheltered development environment for far too long without receiving any input or feedback from the real world outside where the product eventually needs to find its place and make money. These entrepreneurs often refer to their startup as being in 'stealth' mode and claim that someone might steal their idea. We certainly understand their point, but again, nobody can judge the attractiveness of a product better than the real user.

We have seen startups that seem to want to be all things to all people. They offer a wide range of products, features, or options for customization or products for the consumer mass-market alongside products for small and medium-size enterprises and corporate clients. They underestimate the fact that routes to market for these diverse market segments are completely different, as is the message to the market, and they often send out confusing messages to both the market and the investor. This approach will lead to a terrible dilution of resources, which eventually will be spread too thin with the inevitable consequence that nothing will be done well or get done at all.

We have also seen startups that focus on entering many countries or territories at the same time when the focus should be on getting a foothold in one market first and grow outside the home market in a second stage, scaling the business by building on the early success in the home market.

The reasons behind these types of behaviors seem to follow the same pattern: the intent to boil the ocean despite the obvious lack of resources, rather than putting razor-sharp focus on the most important tasks at hand at each point in time.

To avoid that risk of doing too many things while being spread to thin, investors look for some kind of roadmaps:

- **A technology roadmap** - a sequence of product releases outlining new functionalities to be launched over time.
- **A growth roadmap** - the market segments and geographic regions the company will target as it grows, one stage at a time.
- **A roadmap to build out the company** - the headcount, structure, locations, sales representatives, and channels as they evolve over time.
- **A funding roadmap** - an outline of the funding requirements and runway for each funding round to financially back the roadmaps mentioned above.

These roadmaps naturally are not cast in stone and will evolve and change over time. Still, the investor should expect from any entrepreneur to give them some serious thought.

How to Keep Your Team on Track and Get Stuff Done

When it comes to keeping the team on track, it truly has nothing to do with keeping the team busy. A busy team may not always be a successful team. So when it comes to keeping your team on track with the targets and goals of the company, it is all about constructive effort. The team is like an aquarium full of fish. You have to feed them with the dry food of motivation to keep them alive, but rewarding them with worms is equally important. You are not looking for a singular fish to turn big and fat. You want all the fish to grow big together, to make your aquarium look beautiful. We could give you more examples of cleaning the fish tank and how the oxygen pumps are similar to compensation for your team, but let us get to the most important things first.

How to Get Your Fish Tank to Look Beautiful

Your team is your best bet when you want to get things working. So here is what you need to do to get a beautiful aquarium full of fish that are award winning.

- **Stick to the job description:** Don't let Hulk Hogan do the dishes. He would be better at fixing the fences. If you experiment with the strengths of your team too much, then productivity might get lost.

- **Don't count your fish eggs before they hatch:** Sometimes, in extreme enthusiasm and confidence, we often get overambitious and when failure strikes we lose confidence, which takes a lot of time to rebuild within the team. Avoid such occurrences. Be practical about targets and goals for the team.

- **Keep track:** Just as you would keep track of the health of your fish so that you don't lose an entire generation of fish, you need to keep track of your team. After all, a team is as strong as its weakest link. Regular review is the best way to keep everyone at their most productive, tweaking the motivation whenever required.

- **More specification increases efficiency:** Being specific and narrowing down factors involved in the work helps to get exactly what you want from your team. For example, if your team is developing phone-spying software, don't just tell the product name. Explain to them the target audience, the features that you are expecting, the interface, and so on so that you get them moving in the right direction right from the get-go.

- **Scheduling and reaching deadlines:** When you make your team focus on timelines to get the work done, the work gets done. It might be a nightmare for the team but it is something that will keep the team working constructively. Deadlines are like cleaning the fish tank; it helps to bring out the vibrant colors on your fish.

- **Tools and frameworks:** Use all the resources you have for the team. Existing tools, proven processes, and anything else that would maximize productivity should be sought and used. Encourage your team to use the resources, rather than reinventing the wheel each time.

- **Always drop in some food when the fish look beautiful:** Performance incentives and small rewards make a lot of difference to the team and sometimes verbal motivation is not sufficient for enhancing the team's performance. Over-feeding and under-feeding your fish would both affect their health and beauty.

Finally, as a team leader or leader of several teams, in the case of a tech startup always make sure that you practice what you preach. In other words, don't delay your responses and don't stop communicating with your team, or else all targets will be lost.

Lead from the Front and Lead From the Back

"To command is to serve, nothing more and nothing less."
- Andre Malraux

We can tell you a thousand quotes that support this belief, but it is the examples that really matter and prove what we mean by leading from the front and from the back. But first, one needs to be clear about what each of them means. There are two very different kinds of leaders, perhaps two alter egos. The important thing to remember is that leaders aren't perfect. They make mistakes too, just like mere mortals. They need to have the guts to say, "I just stepped on a pile of…animal excrement, avoid this way." But this is only when you are leading from the front. In the world that we live in, it is not enough to be simply reactive to situations; you have to be proactive. This is where leading both from the front and back helps you not only to achieve targets but also make your tech startup big.

Leading from the Front

The tech-startup entrepreneur who leads from the front might be quite like Iron Man: he makes a lot of mistakes but never gives up on his team. Just as Iron Man, AKA Tony Stark, is a philanthropist, an entrepreneur has to lead by example, from the front. He is always the first person to take the hit from enemies. In times of danger, the entrepreneur has to get up there and pave the way for his team to recover. It is quite a task and is always easier said than done.

In the real world, perhaps we most often see people identifying others not as the real life Tony Stark and the real-life Iron Man. Truly, when you are an entrepreneur, you have to imagine yourself as Tony Stark and think what he would have done in this situation. He would be decisive and take the initiative to make things better.

Leading from the Back

When it comes to leading from the back, the aggressive and decisive leader takes a back seat. He puts forward his team and his company. He is measured and patient in his ways of leading his team as well as taking the necessary initiatives. He would be perhaps that person who says, "Now that we have specified the features of the software, go build it."

This does not mean that the leader is not participating in the whole project or is asking his team to do what he is unable to do. Instead, he has enough faith in his team to believe that they will be able to find their way. This requires a lot of confidence and one can only do so if one knows his team inside out.

How Should an Entrepreneur Lead?

Both leading from the front and from the back seem to be contradictory ways of looking at leadership. But it is possible to do both.

The best way to explain it would be through the works of Mahatma Gandhi. He had played the most crucial role for Indian independence. But he took a back seat when it came to being the first political leader of the newly formed republic. Instead of being on the front line, he put his faith in his team members who were able to create one of the most comprehensive constitutions in the world and finally a republican nation within two years. The rest is history. Nelson Mandela is another great example of such dual leadership skills. And, of course, we have Nolan's Batman, if you wish to stay with the superhero examples!

The Company

Setting up a company is relatively easy and straightforward in many countries. However, when a business goes international, things can become rather complex.

Multinational corporations have the financial resources to hire the brightest experts on the planet to advise on company structure and assess the available options from various angles: legal, financial, tax, access to markets, access to finance, and access to talent.

In order to come to grips with deciding which is the best company structure and location, we need to understand what investors are looking for:

- Stable and business/entrepreneur-friendly legislation and administration
- Tax efficiency for both the investor and the entrepreneur
- Proximity to the company's key markets
- Access to funding
- Access to qualified professionals at a reasonable cost
- Aim for a global footprint with presence in major regions

Let us have a closer look at each of these criteria, one by one.

Stable and Business/Entrepreneur-Friendly Legislation and Administration

These requirements encompasses a whole lot of aspects, like the ease and speed of incorporating a company, legislation on corporate governance, administrative and regulatory burdens on doing business, and the legal framework and practices to protect the business and its owners.

Tax Efficiency for Both the Investor and the Entrepreneur

Achieving tax efficiency in international business is a complicated matter due to the lack of harmonization in tax regulation across countries. Many corporates can afford to study legislations of many countries at great length in order to define the most cost-effective tax structure for their company. The fact that physical location has lost relevance in the online business adds significant complication to an already complicated affair.

From an investor's perspective, major consideration has to be given to tax advantages at the time of the investment and the time of the exit, as well as for the case of an involuntary exit (the company going bust).

From a company's perspective, the main focus is on corporate tax, sales tax and VAT, taxes and duties on international trade, taxes and social costs of employment, the availability of R&D, and other tax credits as well as the cost of repatriating profits.

From an entrepreneur's perspective, taxation of capital gains is of overall importance, as well as personal income-related taxes.

Proximity to the Company's Key Markets

Some experts argue that in a connected online world, proximity has lost its importance. That might be true for pure consumer-oriented Internet businesses, but even in that case companies need to take into account local preferences, tastes, languages that affect the products to be offered, pricing decisions, as well as advertising and promotion. Additional consideration has to be given for products that require physical delivery, local representation for sales, distribution, fulfillment, and after-sales service, which in many cases require local proximity.

Access to Funding

As we have seen, many business angels and Venture Capital firms prefer to invest in companies close to their own location. Additional considerations for choosing the right location are the availability of governmental funding, grants, or matching programmes as well as private debt funding.

Access to Qualified Professionals at a Reasonable Cost

Startups, like many other companies, need to attract the best talent and be able to offer attractive remuneration. Given the chronic shortage of cash in the case of startups, the remuneration package often consists of a small fixed component and additional elements with huge upside potential in case of success. Country-specific regulation and taxation rules have to be taken into account in particular for employee share and share option plans.

In addition, talent, although available in many places, tend to concentrate in specific clusters. This makes it easy for companies within a cluster to find talent. However, the downside is that companies and demand for talent concentrate in these clusters too, which can significantly increase the cost of professionals as well as the likelihood of them switching employers. Therefore, extreme care has to be taken in deciding the right location for the team, balancing thoughtfully the costs and associated risks.

Aim for a Global Footprint With Presence in Major Regions

Achieving a global footprint with presence in all major markets should be the aim of any venture-backed business. However, that goal cannot be achieved over night and may take many baby steps along a multi-year journey towards global presence.

Taken into account the many aspects that we have outlined, we therefore recommend any startup to work with experienced advisors who help devise the best strategy and plan. There is no one-size-fits-all and a cookie cutter approach won't do the trick. The plan needs to be tailored to each company's specific characteristics and needs and its execution driven by trusted experts.

AND NOW IT'S UP TO YOU TO MAKE IT HAPPEN!

The Authors

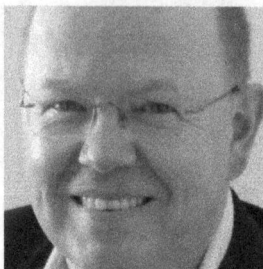

Andreas Bauer

Growth and Innovation Business Partner in Technology, Entrepreneur and Business Executive in Residence, specialized in working hands-on with technology companies to grow their business. Startup champion
helping entrepreneurs to become more
successful in growing their businesses
and getting properly funded..

In the last 20 years he has helped companies, from very small startups at their inception to large blue chip corporations, to grow their business through new product launches and by expanding abroad. His background is truly international, having worked in many countries, including the USA, the UK, Germany, Belgium, Spain, Portugal, Italy and Brazil.

Andreas was lead author of the book "Delivering Superior Service – Reshaping the Communications Service Enterprise", a compendium of thought leadership on IT-enabled bottom-line improvement and top-line growth in the TMT industry.

Andreas promotes growth, entrepreneurship, collaboration, innovation and sustainability through his brand Virtuous Circle Acceleration.

Andreas' business interests include:

International corporate development and execution, through his company four40 Ventures of which he is founder and CEO.

Hot Housing of tech startups, executing growth plans through systematic marketing & sales and channel development.

Virtual Incubation and Acceleration, delivering top-quality mentoring to entrepreneurs around the globe through digital broadcasting and video.

African & Caribbean Community TV, fostering trade, culture, development and education of communities on the African continent and in the Caribbean basin.

Contact
Available to discuss any topic related to growth acceleration, Andreas can be contacted via:

andreas@vcaccel.com (email)
about.me/andreasgbauer (biography)
@andreasgbauer (Twitter)
uk.linkedin.com/pub/andreas-bauer/0/6b9/260/ (LinkedIn)

Julian Hall

#1 Best-selling author, international speaker and award winning serial entrepreneur, Julian Hall is behind the concept of Ultrapreneurship - Making entrepreneurs more successful.

Mentoring entrepreneurs who have gone on to win awards in their own right, Julian has a passion for entrepreneurship and technology and lectures at Universities in London and the Caribbean on the topics. He also coaches entrepreneurs, executives, and CEO's on a weekly basis in the UK and abroad.

In the last 15 years he has consulted and worked for companies big and small, from boot strapped start-ups to blue chip corporations.

Julian travels the globe delivering talks and seminars on innovation, entrepreneurship, dot com and mobile technologies and Ultrapreneurship. He has delivered these talks to audiences in the UK, Europe, USA and the Caribbean.

The author of The 10 Secrets of Social Media Marketing and Entrepreneur to Ultrapreneur - 100 Ways to up Your Game, Julian has achieved Amazon best seller status for both titles. He also coaches authors around the world to publish, market and achieve best seller status.

Julian's companies include:

JulianHall.co.uk – Speaker, Author, Consultant
TheUltrapreneurs.com – Superhero Animation
90DaysToUpYourGame.com – Coaching Programme
UltrapreneurSayings.com – Motivational Sayings
TheOnlineGenius – Digital Agency
The Caribbean Advertising Network – Ad Network
SalmonHallPublishing.com – Book Publishing
ClaimsMasterGroup – Legal sector lead generation

Contact
Available for speaking, workshops, coaching and consultancy, Julian can be contacted via:

genius@julianhall.co.uk (email)
theonlinegenius@gmail.com (email)
julianhall.co.uk (website)
twitter.com/theultrapreneur (Twitter)
facebook.com/theultrapreneur (Facebook)
Linkedin.com/pub/julian-hall/1/9b3/54 (Linkedin)